THE DAILY
WESLEY

Excerpts for Every Day in the Year

Donald E. Demaray, Editor

Bristol House, Ltd.

1993

The Daily Wesley
Excerpts for Every Day in the Year
© Donald E. Demaray, Editor
Published by Bristol House, Ltd.

First Edition, April, 1994

ISBN: 0-917851-80-3

Printed in the United States of America

Bristol House, Ltd.
3131 East 67th Street
Anderson, Indiana 46013

Phone: 317-644-0856
Fax: 317-622-1045
To order call: 1-800-451-READ

In Memory

of my father

C. Dorr Demaray

CREDITS

I must thank Harriet Cook, faithful secretary, and her assistant, Linda Gail Adams, for consistent and genuinely helpful work. Also, I want to express appreciation to William Kostlevy and John Seery, research librarians at Asbury Theological Seminary, both of whom assisted me with joy.

Special thanks go to James Robb and David Cupps of Bristol's editorial staff, both of whom possess gifts of encouragement and know how to press toward goals until accomplished.

My father taught, by living example, the meaning of John Wesley's teachings and the inspired poetry of Charles Wesley's hymns.

TABLE OF CONTENTS

STEADY AND GROWING

John Wesley looked intentionally at the question, How do Christians stay on track and mature? His answer: the means of grace. He listed and explained the five classic channels of grace something like this:

1. **Prayer.** He talked about private, family and public prayer. He said we should play down ourselves and elevate God, pray for others, thank the Almighty for his mercies, and come to grips with our own needs. He asked people to set aside definite times for prayer, morning and evening, and pray before and after we listen to preaching. We should always pray wherever we find ourselves.

2. **Bible Reading.** We must search the Scriptures and do that daily, making notes and always looking at our Bible readings prayerfully. Then we ought to put into practice what we learn. Read, says John Wesley, with your ears open.

3. **The Lord's Supper.** Take it at every opportunity. Prepare prayerfully for it. Take it thoughtfully.

4. **Fasting.** John Wesley thought of fasting in terms of food; today we have medical guides that prevent people with certain diseases from missing meals. But we know, too, that we can fast many ways: from television, from a special event, from spending, from whatever the Spirit of God indicates. Fasting of any type renews our security in God himself and often

provides added time for devotion. Early Christians and early Methodists practiced regular fasting.

5. **Christian Conversation,** what Wesley called "Christian Conference." We must talk graciously, constructively and always with an aim to be vehicles of help to others. Talking too much or too long can produce sinful talk (gossip, slander). Prayer will make us purposeful in conversation. Small groups, conferences, and what today we call seminars, John Wesley would encourage.

PREFACE

John Wesley's ambitious outreach to people saw him travel as much as 20,000 miles a year by horseback, speak to crowds up to 20,000, preach 800 sermons annually and sail to America. He seemed always to have pen in hand, and over a lifetime produced more than 400 separate works (editions totaling over 2,000). His writings, always aimed to touch people exactly where they lived, ranged across the spectrum of life—spiritual and emotional health, music and science, how to cure diseases and stay well. Some of the writings appeared in brief tract form, others in longer books, still others as editions of Christian classics. And he never tired of writing letters to help, encourage and correct the people God sent him, not to mention keeping an extensive journal.

John Wesley gave printers plenty of business, but finally he purchased his own press to hasten distribution and enhance efficiency.

Wesley perceived prayer as high adventure, and would have said a hearty amen to Augustine's conviction that Christians, because they believe in the empty tomb and victory over evil, are Hallelujah People. One never fails to sense Wesley's sustained enthusiasm; indeed, it becomes contagious when reading him.

This is even more true when looking at bite-sized segments, for today we live busy lives without time for long, involved reading. Each reading in this present book takes but a few minutes.

In editing Wesley, I have abbreviated to avoid, insofar as possible, characteristic eighteenth-century elongated writing. I have also replaced older, obscure terms with contemporary words while attempting to stay true to Wesley's intentional meaning. Some materials from John's brother Charles—especially hymns (which John edited)—are included, but most of *The Daily Wesley* stays with John himself, the father of the Methodist movement.

This work introduces people to gospel truth in simple, basic form, and also provides renewed inspiration for those established in the faith. Wesley's rich, practical application of the Bible and clear perception of how life works best will strike readers immediately.

This practical understanding of the gospel makes Wesley one of our best resources for discipling Christians and nurturing people of all ages and classes in earnest about their faith. John Wesley served as a Christian minister to children and youth, as well as people in mid-life and old age. He started a boys' school in an age of illiteracy, had a passion to assist the poor (even helping persons get started in business with a loan fund), the ill (he set up clinical facilities and sometimes served more people than the doctors), and the destitute (he helped individuals get coal for heat, clothes for their bodies, housing for shelter).

The bottom line: Love acted out is the essence of Methodism. And just there lies the reason the love motif surfaces ever and again in Wesley's writings. You will see that as you move, day by day, through the 365 days of the year.

The freshness and creativity of the Wesleys stimulate our reach for God and truth, thereby enriching life as we strive toward the mark of the high calling in Christ Jesus.

Donald E. Demaray
Pentecost Season 1994

Week One

I went to America
to convert the Indians,
but Oh! who will convert me?

John Wesley

PEACE IN THE STORM

We had a big storm which made us batten down
the hatches, the sea breaking over the ship non-stop. I
was at first afraid, but cried to God and was strength-
ened. Before ten, I went to bed; thank God, without fear.
About midnight we were awakened by a confused noise
of seas and wind and men's voices, the like of which I had
never heard before. The sound of the sea breaking over
and against the sides of the ship, I could only compare
with large cannon or American thunder. The rebound-
ing, jerking, quivering motion of the ship resembled
what I had read about earthquakes.

The captain went on deck immediately, but his men
could hear not a single word he said. Clearly we were in
a full-blown hurricane, which began at the southwest,
then went west, northwest, north, and in a quarter of an
hour around by the east to the southwest once more.
The sea churned itself as high as mountains, and from
different points all at once. No wonder the ship would
not obey the helm! The helmsman could not even see
the compass, so violent did the rain come; he just quit
trying to steer the vessel, but in half an hour the stress
of the storm came to a stop.

—John Wesley's *Journal,* January 13, 1738,
on the way home from America

OH! WHO WILL CONVERT ME?

went to America to convert the Indians, but oh! who will convert me? Who will deliver me from my evil heart? I have a fair summer religion. I talk well and I believe when no danger threatens; but let death look me in the face and my spirit troubles me. I cannot say, "To die is gain!"

"I have a sin of fear, that when I've spun my last thread, I shall perish on the shore!"

. . . Anyone who knows me realizes I want to be a real Christian. My lifestyle shows that. I am even content to let people criticize me. But in a storm, I ask myself, What if the gospel isn't true? That's why I am, of all men, most foolish. Well then, what on earth is the real meaning of my Christian experience? It's only a dream, a mere fable.

Oh! who will deliver me from this fear of death? What shall I do? Where shall I go? What kind of decision shall I make? A man of wisdom advised me to quiet myself and go on. Perhaps he's right. I could look on the confusion as my cross; when it comes, I can simply let it humble me and renew all my good intentions, especially praying without ceasing. At other times, I could pay no attention to the inner thoughts, just quietly go on doing God's work.

—John Wesley's *Journal*, January 24, 1738

ALDERSGATE (1)

What occurred on Wednesday, 24th (May), I think best to relate in context, making it better understood. If you cannot identify with what follows, ask the God of light to give you more light, and me too. [John Wesley relates the context of his conversion in 16 numbered sections of the *Journal.*]

1. I believe, until I was about ten years old, I had not sinned away the Holy Spirit's washing given me in baptism, having been strictly educated and carefully taught that I could be saved only by obedience in everything, by keeping all the commandments of God—and I was instructed diligently in the meaning of those commandments. And the instructions, as they related to outward duties and sins, I gladly received and often thought about. But everything that was said about inward obedience or holiness, I neither understood nor remembered. This made me as ignorant of the true meaning of the law as I was of the gospel of Christ.

—John Wesley's *Journal*, May 24, 1738

ALDERSGATE (2)

2. The next six or seven years I spent at school. There, outward restraints were removed, and I was much more negligent than before, even of obvious duties. Almost continually I was guilty of sins I knew were clearly wrong. These sins were not scandalous from the world's point of view, and I still read the Scriptures and said my prayers both morning and evening. And I now hoped to be saved by (1) not being so bad as others, (2) having a kindly heart toward religion, and (3) reading the Bible, attending church and saying my prayers.

—John Wesley's *Journal,* May 24, 1738

ALDERSGATE (3)

3. Away at university for five years, I continued to say my prayers both in public and in private. And I read the Scriptures; also several other books of a religious sort, especially comments on the New Testament. Yet in all this, I had not so much as a single idea about inward holiness. In fact, I went on habitually, and for the most part contentedly, in known sins. I had some intermissions in my sinning, and short struggles, especially before and after Holy Communion, which I had to receive three times a year. I cannot tell you how I hoped to be saved, since I sinned continually even against the little light I had. Perhaps I thought my transient fits of repentance, as some preachers taught, would save me.

—John Wesley's *Journal*, May 24, 1738

ALDERSGATE (4)

4. **W**hen I was about 22 years of age, my father pressed me to begin the ordination process. At the same time, the providence of God directed me to read Thomas à Kempis' *Imitation of Christ.* In that book, I began to see that true religion was seated in the heart and that God's law extended to all our thoughts, words and actions. I was, however, very angry with à Kempis for being *too strict.* . . . Yet, I got a lot of real comfort reading him, and learned things to which I was an utter stranger before.

At the same time, I began meeting with a Christian friend—I had never had such fellowship before—and I now changed my whole style of conversation. I set out in earnest on "a new life." I scheduled an hour or two a day for quiet time. I took Holy Communion every week. I kept a keen eye against all sin, whether in word or deed. I began to aim at, and pray for, inward holiness. No wonder, *doing so much and living so good a life,* I believed I had arrived at being a good Christian.

—John Wesley's *Journal,* May 24, 1738

ALDERSGATE (5)

5. **M**oving soon after to another college, I put into practice a resolution I had been convinced was of utmost importance—shaking off immediately all trifling activities. I saw more and more the value of time. I applied myself closer to study. I kept an eye out against actual sins; I advised others to be religious, according to the scheme of religion by which I modeled my own life. But meeting now with Mr. Law's *Christian Perfection* and *Serious Call* (although I was much offended at many parts of both books), they convinced me more than ever of the exceeding height and breadth and depth of the law of God. The light flowed in so strongly upon my soul that everything appeared in a new way. I cried to God for help, and resolved not to prolong the time of obeying him, and to obey as I had never done before. I determined, by continued endeavor, to keep God's whole law, inward and outward, to the very best of my ability. I was persuaded that I should be accepted by him and that I was then saved.

—John Wesley's *Journal,* May 24, 1738

Week Two

❧

I was too learned and too wise,
so it all seemed foolishness to me.

I was *striving with*, not
freed from, sin.

John Wesley

ALDERSGATE (6)

6. In 1730 I began visiting the prisons, assisting
the poor and sick in town, and doing what other good I
could by my presence or by what little money I had, to
help both the bodies and souls of people. In order to do
these things, I revised my lifestyle to refuse luxuries,
even what many call necessities. Soon people used my
name as slang for self-denial, and I was glad that my
name was smudged by the world.

The next spring I began fasting on Wednesdays and
Fridays, commonly done in the ancient church, tasting
no food until three P.M. But now I didn't know the next
step to take. I diligently strove against all sin. I over-
looked no self-denial I thought good. For that reason I
suffered evil. And all this I knew to be nothing, unless it
was directed toward inward holiness. Accordingly, this
holiness—the image of God—I aimed at in everything I
did, trying to do his will, not mine.

Yet trying this for some years, I saw myself near
death; all this effort gave me no comfort or assurance of
acceptance with God. This awareness took me very
much by surprise. Had I been building on the sand? I
hadn't yet understood that the true foundation cannot
be laid by a person, but only God, only Jesus Christ.

—John Wesley's *Journal*, May 24, 1738

ALDERSGATE (7)

7. **S**oon after, a contemplative man convinced me, even more than ever, that outward works amount to nothing in themselves. In several conversations he instructed me how to pursue inward holiness, union of the soul with God. But about his instructions, though I received them as words from God, I must observe (a) that he spoke so incautiously against trust in outward works that he discouraged me from doing them at all; (b) that he recommended, as if to supply what was missing, mental prayer and similar exercises, as the most effective ways of purifying the soul and unifying it with God. Now these were, in point of fact, as much my own works as visiting the sick or clothing the naked. "Union with God," then, was as truly my own righteousness as any effort I had tried before under another name.

—John Wesley's *Journal,* May 24, 1738

ALDERSGATE (8)

8. In this refined way of trusting to my own works and my own righteousness, so zealously urged by the mystic writers, I dragged on heavily, finding no comfort or help until I left England. On shipboard I was again active in outward works. On board, God, in his mercy, gave me twenty-six Moravians for companions; they endeavored to show me a more excellent way. But I didn't understand it at first. I was too learned and too wise, so it all seemed foolishness to me. And I continued preaching and following after, and trusting in, *works* righteousness, righteousness that can justify no one.

—John Wesley's *Journal*, May 24, 1738

ALDERSGATE (9)

9. The whole time at Savannah I was beating the air. I was ignorant of the righteousness of Christ, which, by a living faith in him, brings salvation to every one who believes. I tried to establish my own righteousness, and therefore labored in the fire all the time. I was properly *under the law.* I knew that the law of God was spiritual; I recognized that it was good. I even delighted in it from my heart. Yet I was carnal, sold a bill of goods by sin. Every day I was constrained to cry out, I do what I don't want to; what I want to do, I don't do; what I hate, I do. I will to do the right things, but I have not found out how to do what my will wants. For the good I want to do, I don't do. And the evil I don't want to do, I do. There seems to be a law inside me that says when I want to do good, evil is present with me. So the law of my person wars against the law of my mind, and brings me into captivity to the law of sin.

—John Wesley's *Journal,* May 24, 1738

ALDERSGATE (10)

10. In this state of mind I fought continually, but never conquered. Before, I had willingly served sin; now it was unwillingly, but still I served it. I fell and rose, and fell again. Sometimes I was overcome and in heaviness: sometimes I overcame and was happy. Rules made me feel imprisoned; the gospel made me feel comforted. During this whole struggle between nature and grace— the struggle continued about 10 years—I had many remarkable returns to the life of prayer, especially when I was in trouble. I was aware of many helps, clearly short hints of the liberation of faith. But I was still *under the law*, not *under grace*. My state then was really where most Christians are content to live and die: I was *striving with*, not *freed from*, sin. Nor did I have the witness of the Spirit with my spirit, and indeed could not, for I did not seek it *by faith*, but by the works of the law.

—John Wesley's *Journal*, May 24, 1738

ALDERSGATE (11)

11. During my return to England, January 1738, being in real danger of death and very uneasy, I was strongly convinced that the cause of that uneasiness was unbelief, and that the true and living faith was the one thing I must have. But still I fixed my eye not on this faith with its true object: I focused only on faith in God, not on faith through Christ. I did not know I was completely without *this faith;* I thought I had enough of this faith.

So when Peter Böhler, whom God prepared for me as soon as I came to London, affirmed true faith in Christ —there is only one such faith—I was told it had two fruits, which always stay together like Siamese twins: "dominion over sin, and constant peace from a sense of forgiveness." I was quite amazed at this, and looked at it as a new gospel. If this was so, clearly I did not have faith.

But I was not willing to be convinced of this. Therefore I argued with all my might and labored to prove that faith lived in a different place, especially where the sense of forgiveness did not live; for all the Scriptures relating to this I had been taught all along to rationalize away. . . . Besides, I saw easily that, in the nature of things, no one could really have this sense of forgiveness and not *feel* it. But I didn't feel it. If, then, I really didn't have faith without this, I was only pretending faith.

—John Wesley's *Journal,* May 24, 1738

ALDERSGATE (12)

12. **W**hen I met Peter Böhler again, he consented to a debate on my issue: Scripture and experience. I first consulted Scripture. But when I set aside the interpretations of people and simply considered the words of God, and comparing text with text, endeavoring to illustrate the obscure passages by the plain ones, I discovered the Bible was really against me, and I had to retreat to my last stronghold. That last stronghold? I could not say yes to Scripture until I found living witnesses to prove it.

Peter Böhler replied that he could show me living witnesses any time, even the next day. So the next day he came to see me with three people, all of whom testified of their own personal experience that a true living faith in Christ is inseparable from a sense of pardon for all the past, and freedom from all present sins. They added, with one accord, that this faith was the gift, the free gift of God, and that he would surely give it to every soul who earnestly and perseveringly sought it.

I was not thoroughly convinced, and, by God's grace, resolved to seek it till I found it. First, by absolutely renouncing all dependence *on my own* works or righteousness—on which I had really built my hope of salvation, even though I did not really know salvation, from my youth up. Second, I determined to seek grace by adding to the constant use of the other means of grace—including continual prayer for this very faith—justifying, saving faith, a full reliance on the blood of Christ shed for *me*, a trust in him as *my* Christ, as *my* only justification, sanctification, and redemption.

—John Wesley's *Journal*, May 24, 1738

Week Three

About a quarter before nine, while he was describing the change which God works in the heart through faith in Christ, I felt my heart strangely warmed.

. . . now I was always conqueror.

John Wesley

ALDERSGATE (13)

13. I continued to seek this faith, though with strange indifference, dullness, and coldness, with unusually frequent relapses into sin. I continued this way until Wednesday, May 24. I think it was about five this morning, that I opened my New Testament on the words about exceeding great and precious promises, and that we should be partakers of the divine nature (2 Peter 1:4). Just as I was about to leave my apartment, I reopened my Testament again, and read, "You are not far from the kingdom of God." In the afternoon, I was asked to go to St. Paul's. The anthem was "Out of the deep have I called unto you, O Lord; Lord, hear my voice. O let my ears consider well the voice of my complaint. If you, Lord, will be extreme to mark what is done amiss, O Lord, who may abide it? For there is mercy with you; therefore shall you be feared. O Israel, trust in the Lord, for with the Lord there is mercy and with him is plenteous redemption. And he shall redeem Israel from all his sins."

—John Wesley's *Journal*, May 24, 1738

ALDERSGATE (14)

14. In the evening, I went very unwillingly to a society in Aldersgate Street, where one was reading Luther's Preface to his commentary on the Epistle to the Romans. About a quarter before nine, while he was describing the change that God works in the heart through faith in Christ, I felt my heart strangely warmed. I felt I did trust in Christ, Christ alone for salvation; and an assurance was given me that he had taken away *my* sins, even *mine*, and saved *me* from the law of sin and death.

—John Wesley's *Journal*, May 24, 1738

ALDERSGATE (15)

15. began to pray with all my might for those who had in a special way despitefully used me and persecuted me. I then testified openly to all there what I now first felt in my heart. But it was not long before the enemy suggested, "This cannot be faith, for where is your joy?" Then I learned that peace and victory over sin are essential to faith in my Savior, but that as to the transports of joy that usually come at the beginning of faith, especially in those who have mourned deep, God sometimes gives, sometimes withholds them, determined by his own will.

—John Wesley's *Journal,* May 24, 1738

ALDERSGATE (16)

16. After my return home, I experienced many temptations. But I cried out, and they went away. They returned again and again. I lifted my eyes to the Lord every time. God sent me help from heaven. And just there I discovered the difference between my present and former states; namely, so long as I fought sometimes under law, sometimes under grace, I was often conquered, but now I was always conqueror.

—John Wesley's *Journal,* May 24, 1738

LOVE GOD SUPREMELY

The most spiritually fit person is the one who knows, by experience, the full force of that glorious rule, "Set your affections on things above, and not on things of the earth." Don't you think that means the same as, "You shall love the Lord your God with all your heart, soul, and strength"? But what do we mean by loving God? Isn't loving to delight habitually? So then, the real thrust of both verses is this—to delight in the Creator more than in his creatures, to take more pleasure in God than in anything he made, to rejoice in nothing so much as in serving him. Pascal observed that most people use God and enjoy the world; but Christians do quite the opposite—they use the world while they enjoy God.

—John Wesley, *Letters,* to Mrs. Pendarves,
February 11, 1731

DELIVER ME FROM SELF-LOVE

bove all, deliver me, O my God, from the idolatry of self-love. I know, Lord (thank you for letting me know), that this is the root of all evil. I know you made me not to do my own will but yours. I know the essence of demonic perversion is a will against yours. So do be my helper against this most dangerous of all idols, that I may both discern all its subtleties and stand securely against its force. You command me to substitute your will for mine, so give me strength to obey your command. I ask that your almighty arm establish me, put steel into me, and settle me so you will always be the solid ground and pillar of my love.

—John Wesley, *A Collection of Forms of Prayer
for Every Day in the Week,* 1738

TO TASTE YOUR LOVE
IS ALL MY CHOICE!

Each moment draw from earth away
  My heart, that lowly waits your call:
Speak to my inner soul, and say,
  "I am your Love, your God, your All!"
To feel your power, to hear your voice,
  To taste your love is all my choice!

—John Wesley's translation from the German of a
Gerhard Tersteegen hymn (1697-1769)

You may wish to read aloud the Wesley hymns to catch their deep meanings, carried along by the lilt, beauty and rhythm.

Week Four

❧

Love makes a Christian rejoice in the virtues of all . . . sympathize with their pains and show compassion for their weaknesses.

John Wesley

JOHN WESLEY'S
COVENANT SERVICE (1)

ix three principles in your heart: (1) Eternal
matters weigh considerably more than earthly matters;
(2) In reality, what you cannot see is as certain as what
you can see; (3) Your choice right now determines your
eternal destiny.

Choose Christ and his ways; this will bring you
blessing. Refuse Christ, and you miss happiness forever.

As you make your choice, notice carefully the distinction between the right and the left:

Christ gives you his yoke, his cross, his crown.
The devil gives you wealth, pleasure, and a curse.

Now that you see clearly the difference, say to yourself, "My soul, you have the alternatives before you;
what will you choose? Will you have the crown or the
curse? If you choose the crown, you must content yourself to submit to the Cross and the yoke, the service and
the sufferings of Christ—all linked to each other. So
what do you say? Would you rather take the gains and
pleasures of sin, and gamble on the curse? Or will you
yield yourself as a servant to Christ and in this way
make your crown certain?"

—John Wesley, original *Covenant Service*, 1790;
quotations from 1809 edition (London)

COVENANT (2)

If your heart fails you, and you hesitate at the business of making a decision, stop yourself immediately. To say you will make no decision is to make a decision; to remain undetermined for Christ is to determine for the devil. Therefore, don't weaken, but resolve in your heart. Do not let your thoughts rest until you face that issue, then see that you make the right choice.

To do that means to choose good, God and happiness in the world to come. This involves renouncing the world and its happiness.

—John Wesley, original *Covenant Service,* 1790; quotations from 1809 edition (London)

COVENANT (3)

mbark with Christ. Venture out on him. Cast yourself on his goodness, knowing that will bring you to God . . . like a poor captive exile on a strange island, an island of robbers and murderers. You have no hope of living there or escaping to your home. But at length you meet a pilot who offers you safe transportation back home. You get on board with him and venture all that you have on him and his ship.

Your sins are robbers, your pleasures are robbers, your companions in sin, robbers and thieves. To stay with them means to perish. Christ offers to take you safely home.

That's why you must pray, "Lord Jesus, take care of me. Bring me to God. Take me to the Land of Promise. With you I venture; I surrender myself to yourself and your blood. I trust your goodness. I put all my hopes in you."

Now this is "closing" with Christ your Priest. This means you renounce your own goodness, since your own goodness cannot save you.

—John Wesley, original *Covenant Service,* 1790;
quotations from 1809 edition (London)

COVENANT (4)

ou must face two realities in order to come to
Christ. (1) A deep sense of your sin and misery. No one
can take the Savior seriously who does not see oneself a
sinner. (Why does a well person need to go to the doctor?) The Holy Spirit, to save the world, must convince
people of sin (John 16:8). That is, he brings sins before
one's eyes and conscience. This makes people feel abomi-
nable. Sin hides itself with all its vileness and deformity.
But God's Spirit takes off the mask and makes sin look
like sin, makes the sinner's gods appear as so many
devils, and brings the blackness and filth of sin to sight.
With all this, the guilt of sin comes into view and sets
all these devils to tormenting the sinner, bringing fear,
terror and amazement. That's why we sometimes call
the Holy Spirit the Spirit of Bondage. The Spirit awak-
ens sleepy sinners, a kind of awakening in hell. Sinners
ask, "What's the meaning of all this? Have I been a mere
party goer, making merry, while my soul lives in such a
wretched state? I'm dead if I continue like this!"

When one comes to this, Christ has a chance at us.
But for the second reality: (2) An utter despair of oneself
and all things except Christ. Aware of sin and danger,
the sinner looks for help, for deliverance. But one looks
everywhere before looking to Christ. Nothing will bring
the sinner to Christ but absolute necessity. The sinner
will *try* to stop drinking and *try* to terminate adultery
just to see if self-saving is possible. Even prayers, sermons and sacraments become attempted savior-substi-
tutes; though good in themselves, they cannot save!
One's righteousness (just rags!) can't save; one's duties

41

cannot. Rules and regulations won't save. Knock on any of these doors only to find no salvation.

Then what will I do? Giving away all I have, even my body to be burned, won't save my soul. To come to this distress, this utter loss, this despair—that drives me to the Savior.

—John Wesley, original *Covenant Service,* 1790; quotations from 1809 edition (London)

COVENANT (5)

To come now to Christ, you will notice three guarantees:

1. God's chosen Son: He sent Jesus to the world to rescue sinners. The chosen, saving Person is Jesus. God commissioned Jesus to save. As Isaiah 53 says, God put his Spirit on him.

2. God's Summons. 1 John 3:23: "This is his commandment, that we should believe on the name of his Son, Jesus Christ."

3. The Promise of God. I Peter 2:6: "Behold! I lay in Zion a chief Cornerstone, elect, precious; those who believe on him shall not go wrong."

Now having this threefold guarantee, the guarantee of God's choosing, summons and promise, you may boldly adventure with Christ, saying, "Lord Jesus, here I am, a poor captive exile, lost, an enemy of God. Please, Lord, help me, reconcile me to God, save my soul."

—John Wesley, original *Covenant Service*, 1790;
quotations from 1809 edition (London)

COVENANT (6)

Resign yourself to God in Christ. Surrender yourself to the Lord as his servant. Give up the dominion and government of yourself. "Don't yield your members as instruments of unrighteousness and sin, but surrender yourselves to God, as people alive from the dead, and your members as instruments of righteousness to God. Yield yourselves to God as servants who obey."

From now on identify with the Lord. "I am yours," says the psalmist. But those who give themselves to sin and the world, really say, "Sin, I am yours; World, I am yours; Riches, I am yours; Pleasures, I am yours."

—John Wesley, original *Covenant Service*, 1790; quotations from 1809 edition (London)

COVENANT (7)

This giving of yourself to God, means you enthusiastically content yourself to his appointment for your work. He can put you anywhere he pleases. Servants do what their master assigns. They identify with any work he assigns. They cannot pick and choose, saying, "I will do this and not that; this is too hard; that is beneath me; or that would be better not done at all." Good servants, having chosen their master, let the master choose their work and will not dispute his will; they will just do it.

Christ needs many things done. Some come with ease and honor, others with difficulty and even disgrace. Some come suitable to our gifts and interest, others contrary to both. In some we please both Christ and ourselves—example: feeding and clothing ourselves. Some spiritual duties strike us as more pleasing—example: rejoicing in the Lord, feeding ourselves with the comforts and delights of religion. But other works include pleasing Christ by lending, giving, putting up with others, reproving people of their sins, withdrawing from their company, witnessing against their wickedness, confessing Christ at the cost of shame and reproach, parting from ease and accommodations for the name of our Lord, Jesus.

—John Wesley, original *Covenant Service*, 1790;
quotations from 1809 edition (London)

Week Five

If he is a Father, then he is
good, then he is loving
to his children.

John Wesley

COVENANT (8)

onsider carefully the cost of serving Christ. Take
a thorough survey of the whole business of Christianity.

First, see what Christ expects, and yield yourself to
his whole will. Do not try to make your own terms;
Christ will never allow that.

Second, ask the Lord to make you what he will and
put you where he wishes. He can make you silver or
gold, wood or stone; higher or lower, finer or coarser;
head, ear or eye; hard working, or contemptible; in the
wilderness or with woodcutters, drawers of water, the
doorkeepers of his house . . . anywhere. He can put me to
what he will, rank me with whom he will, put me to
doing or to suffering, employed for God or laid aside for
him exalted for him or trodden under foot for him. I can
be full or empty, have all things or nothing. I freely and
heartily resign all to God's pleasure and disposal.

—John Wesley, original *Covenant Service,* 1790;
quotations from 1809 edition (London)

COVENANT (9)

The essence of Christianity lies in the kind of closure with Christ we've talked about. This closure means you make Christ King and sovereign Lord. In this, you renounce the *devil* and his works, the flesh and its lusts. You consent to all the laws and orders of Christ and his spiritual government.

You have chosen the sinless crown when you make God your everything and happiness, when you venture your whole interest on him with all your hopes. Christ can be the Savior only of his servants. He is the Author of Salvation to those who obey him. Christ will have no servants except by consent. His people are a willing people. He will be all in all, or he will be nothing.

—John Wesley, original *Covenant Service,* 1790;
quotations from 1809 edition (London)

COVENANT (10)

How do we actually put the covenant into practice? Let me make these suggestions: (1) Set apart some time, more than once, to spend in secret before the Lord. In that quiet time, earnestly seek his special assistance; look carefully at the distinct conditions of the covenant; search your heart to determine whether you have already decided for Christ; look at your own sins and at God's laws. Make your choice.

(2) Put yourself into the most serious frame of mind, suitable to a transaction of the highest importance.

(3) Lay hold on the covenant of God, rely on his promise of grace and strength to follow through on your promise. Don't trust your own strength, or the strength of your resolutions, but take hold of his strength.

(4) Resolve to live faithfully. Having engaged your heart, now say out loud what you will do, and then put your hands to work to act out your intention.

(5) Having now prepared yourself, fall on your knees, lift your open hands to heaven, and talk to the Lord like this:

"Almighty God, Searcher of hearts, you know that I make this covenant today, with no known guile or reservation, asking that if you see any flaw or falsehood in me that you let me know about it, and help me to put it right. And now, from this day on, I look to you as my God and Father. You have washed away my sins; you are now my Savior and Redeemer. Glory to you, O God, who by your finger, turned my heart from sin to you. Amen."

—John Wesley, original *Covenant Service*, 1790;
quotations from 1809 edition (London)

COVENANT (11)

This Covenant I advise you to make not only in your heart, but in word; not only in word, but in writing. I suggest, too, that with all possible reverence, you spread the writing before the Lord, as an act and deed. When you have done this, sign on the dotted line. Keep this document in your lock box, so you can take it out and look at it when doubts and temptations come. Then celebrate with this hymn:

> Come, let us use the grace divine,
>> And all with one accord,
> In a perpetual Covenant join
>> Ourselves to Christ the Lord.
> Give us ourselves, through Jesus' power,
>> His name to glorify;
> And promise in this sacred hour,
>> For God to live and die.
> The Cov'nant we this moment make,
>> Be ever kept in mind:
> We will no more our God forsake,
>> Or cast his words behind.
> We never will throw off his fear,
>> Who hears our solemn vow:
> And if thou art well pleas'd to hear,
>> Come down, and meet us now!
> Thee, Father, Son, and Holy Ghost,
>> Let all our hearts receive!
> Present with the celestial host,
>> The peaceful answer give!

To each the Cov'nant blood apply,
 Which takes our sins away;
And register our names on high,
 And keep us to that day!

—John Wesley, original *Covenant Service*, 1790;
quotations from 1809 edition (London)

GROUP BENEFITS

Toward the end of the year 1739, eight or ten persons came to me in London; they appeared to be deeply convinced of sin, and earnestly struggling for redemption. They desired (as did two or three more the next day) that I spend time with them in prayer, and advise them how to flee from the wrath to come, which they saw always hanging over their heads. So we could have more time for this very important work, I set aside a weekly period on Thursday evening. The number increased daily. I gave counsel, the kind I perceived they needed most. We always concluded our meeting with prayer shaped to meet their personal needs.

The United Society groups started in London and then in other places. This kind of society is "a company of men having the form and seeking the power of godliness, united in order to pray together, to receive the word of exhortation, and to watch over one another in love, that they may help each other to work out their salvation."

—John Wesley, "The Nature, Design, and General Rules of the United Societies, in London, Bristol, Kingswood, Newcastle-Upon-Tyne," 1743

FLEE THE WRATH TO COME

People join the societies under just one condition —a desire to flee from the wrath to come, to be saved from their sins. When people really establish this in their souls, fruit always appears. So we expect all who continue in the societies to show evidence of their salvation.

First, by doing no harm, by avoiding evil of every kind, especially that most generally practiced. Such as, taking God's name in vain, taking a secularist attitude toward Sunday... drunkenness, buying or selling liquor, drinking (except for medical reasons), fighting, quarreling, stirring up a ruckus, brother going to court against brother, returning evil for evil, criticizing one another, using many words in buying and selling, buying and selling black-market products, charging exorbitant interest rates, unkind and unprofitable conversation (such as gossiping about government leaders), breaking the golden rule, excessive dress, diversions Jesus would not participate in, music and reading that doesn't please God, softness and needless self-indulgence, laying up treasures on earth, borrowing without knowing you can pay back.

—John Wesley, "The Nature, Design, and General
Rules of the United Societies, in London, Bristol,
Kingswood, Newcastle-Upon-Tyne," 1743

POSITIVE EVIDENCE
OF SALVATION

We expect all who continue in the societies to show positive evidence of their desire for salvation.

How? By doing good, showing mercy in every way and to everybody insofar as possible, giving food to the hungry, clothing the naked, visiting and helping the sick, doing the same for people in prison. We also expect our people to minister to souls by instructing, reproving, exhorting those they contact, trampling the view that says we are not to do good unless we feel like it.

We also do good to Christians or those searching. We should employ them first, buy from them, help them in business—this especially because the world helps its own and only them. More, we must be diligent stewards so that people don't blame the gospel. We run with patience the race set before us, deny ourselves, take up the cross every day. We also prepare ourselves to get criticized for Christ . . . even expect that people will say all sorts of evil things against us for the Lord's sake.

We also assume our society people will attend worship, listen to the preaching of the Word and read the Bible. We expect them to take the Lord's Supper, have family and private prayer, search the Scriptures, fast, and exercise discipline.

—John Wesley, "The Nature, Design, and General
Rules of the United Societies, in London, Bristol,
Kingswood, Newcastle-Upon-Tyne," 1743

Week Six

At five I preached once more on
"Believe on the Lord Jesus Christ,
and you will be saved."
They all devoured the Word. Oh,
may that Word give them
health for their souls and marrow
for strong bones!

John Wesley

OUR FATHER

In commenting on the first words of the Lord's prayer, John Wesley says:

Our Father: If he is a Father, then he is good, he is loving to his children. And here is the first and great reason for prayer. God is willing to bless; let us ask for a blessing. *Our Father:* Our Creator; the Author of our being; he who raised us from the dust of the earth; who breathed into us the breath of life, and we became living souls. But if he made us, let us ask, and he will not withhold any good thing from the work of his own hands. *Our Father:* Our Preserver; who, day by day, sustains the life he has given; of whose continuing love we now and every moment receive life and breath and all things. So much the more boldly let us come to him, and we shall obtain mercy, and find grace to help in time of need. Above all, the Father of our Lord Jesus Christ, and of all that believe in him; who justifies us freely by his grace, through the redemption that is in Jesus; who has blotted out all our sins, and healed all our infirmities; who has received us for his own children, by adoption and grace; and, because we are sons and daughters, has sent forth the Spirit of his son into our hearts, crying, Abba, Father; who has given us second birth from seed not capable of rotting, and created us new in Christ Jesus. Therefore we know that he hears us always; therefore we pray to him without ceasing. We pray, because we love; and we love him because he first loved us.

—John Wesley's sermon, "Upon Our Lord's Sermon on the Mount, VI," 1748

FORGIVENESS

About the expression, "As we forgive those who trespass against us," John Wesley said:

In these words our Lord clearly declares both on what condition, and in what degree or manner, we may expect to be forgiven by God. All our trespasses and sins are forgiven us, *if* we forgive others. This is a point of the utmost importance. Our blessed Lord is so concerned that we not let it slip out of our thoughts that he not only puts it in the body of the Lord's prayer, but after the prayer repeats it. "If," he says, "you forgive men their trespasses, your heavenly Father will also forgive you. But if you don't forgive others, your heavenly Father will not forgive you."

God forgives us as we forgive others. So that if any malice or bitterness, if any taint of unkindness or anger remains, if we do not clearly, fully and from the heart forgive everyone his or her sins, we so far cut short the forgiveness of God for us. God, then, cannot clearly and fully forgive us; he may show us some degree of mercy, but we do not allow him to blot out all our sins and forgive all our iniquities.

If we do not, from our hearts, forgive our neighbor, what kind of prayer are we really offering to God when we say the Lord's Prayer?

—John Wesley's sermon, "Upon Our Lord's
Sermon on the Mount, VI," 1748

LEAD US NOT
INTO TEMPTATION

The word translated *temptation* means trial of any kind. And so the English word "temptation" was formerly taken in a general sense, though now it is usually understood as solicitation to sin. Saint James uses the word in both senses: first, in its general way, then in its more confined way. He takes it in the former sense when he says, "Blessed is the man that endures temptation, for when he is tried, he shall receive the crown of life" (James 1:12). Then James uses the word in the more specific sense: "Let no one say, when he is tempted, I am tempted of God. For God cannot be tempted with evil, neither can he tempt anyone. But every one is tempted when he is drawn by his or her own lust or desire" (verses 13-14). James here talks about being enticed, caught as a fish with bait. Then he enters into temptation. Then temptation covers one like a cloud; it overspreads the whole soul. Then how hard it is to escape the snare! Therefore, we plead with God not to lead us into temptation; that is, not to let us be caught in it.

—John Wesley's sermon, "Upon Our Lord's Sermon on the Mount, VI," 1748

GOD SAVES A DRUNKARD

At five in the evening I preached at Dewsbury and on Friday the 17th I reached Manchester. Here I heard an account of a remarkable incident. A well-known drunkard of Congleton used to curse and swear at the preacher, refusing to listen to the gospel. One evening, however, he stepped inside. What he heard made him so uneasy he could not sleep that night. In the morning, still more upset, he walked the fields, but with no relief. He went to see an old drinking buddy, one always ready to say bad things about the Methodists. But his companion told him to "go join the Methodist society." He went on to say that he himself had never been so uneasy and would join the Methodists, too.

Both men joined right away. But David then said, "I am sorry I joined, for I will get drunk again and the church will turn me out." But he refrained from drink four days; yet, on the fifth, some of his old friends persuaded him to drink. He took a pint, then another, and still another, until one of them said, "See, here is a Methodist drunk!"

David, angered, knocked him to the floor, chair and all. He then drove the others from the house, picked up the landlady and carried her out; went back in and broke down the door, then threw the door into the street. He ran into the fields, tore his hair, and rolled up and down on the ground.

In a day or two he attended a love feast, taking a back seat where no one could see him. While Mr. Furze prayed, David was seized with a dreadful agony, both of body and mind. This caused many to wrestle with God for him. In a while he sprang to his feet, stretched out his hands, and cried, "All my sins are forgiven!" In that instant someone on the other side of the room cried, "Jesus is mine! And he has taken away all my sins." This was Samuel H. David, who burst through the crowd, took David in his arms and said, "Let's sing the Virgin Mary's song. I never could sing it before. 'My soul doth magnify the Lord, and my spirit doth rejoice in God my Savior.' " And what happened next made clear to all that God had really saved them!

—John Wesley's *Journal*, June 17, 1763

BE IN EARNEST

After preaching at Alnwick, I rode on to New-
castle. Certainly if I did not believe there was another
world, I would spend all my summers here; I know no
place in Great Britain comparable to it for pleasantness.
But I seek another country and therefore am content to
be a wanderer on the earth.

I preached at Nafferton at one. While riding to
Nafferton, a woman stopped me on the road. "Sir," she
said, "do you remember when you came to Prudhoe two
years ago and you breakfasted at Thomas Newton's? I
am his sister. You looked at me as you left and said, 'Be
in earnest.' I did not know then what earnestness
meant, nor had I given it any thought at all. But the
words sank into my heart so that I could never rest until
I searched out Christ and found him."

—John Wesley's *Journal,* June 4 and 21, 1759

SPECIFIC TRUTH

I preached at seven in the high school yard, Edinburgh, Scotland. It being the time of the General Assembly of the Church of Scotland, which drew not only the ministers, but nobility and gentry, many of both were present. But a lot more came at five in the afternoon. I spoke as plainly as ever I did in my life. But I never knew any in Scotland offended at plain dealing. In this respect the North Britons are a pattern to all mankind.

God has revived his work in these parts in remarkable ways. A few months ago the people showed precious little life. Samuel Meggot, perceiving this, advised the society at Barnard Castle to observe every Friday with fasting and prayer. The very first Friday they met together, God broke in upon them in a wonderful manner; his work has increased ever since. The neighboring societies heard about what happened and agreed to follow the same rule; soon they experienced the same blessing. To neglect this specific duty (I mean fasting, ranked by our Lord with almsgiving and prayer) is one reason for deadness among Christians. Can anyone willingly neglect it without guilt?

—John Wesley's *Journal,* May 29 and June 7, 1763

GOD'S PROMISE

Christianity promises that godly character shall be mine if I will not rest till I attain it. This is promised both in the Old Testament and in the New. Indeed the New is, in effect, all a promise, because every description of the servants of God mentioned has the nature of a command . . . "Be followers of me, as I am of Christ" (1 Corinthians 11:1); "Be followers of those who through faith and patience inherit the promises" (Hebrews 6:12). And every command has the force of a promise . . . "A new heart will I give you, and I will put my Spirit within you, and cause you to walk in my statutes, and you shall keep my judgments, and do them" (Ezekiel 36:26-27). Accordingly, when we read, "You shall love the Lord your God with all your heart, and with all your soul, and with all your mind" (Matthew 22:37), this not only gives us a direction to go, but a promise of what God will do in me, exactly equivalent with what we read elsewhere: "The Lord your God will circumcise your heart, and the heart of your seed . . . to love the LORD your God with all your heart, and with all your soul" (Deuteronomy 30:6).

—John Wesley, "A Plain Account
of Genuine Christianity," 1753

Week Seven

Will you have the Crown
or the curse?

To say you will make no decision is
to make a decision. . . .

John Wesley

ABOVE ALL, LOVE

Above all remembering that God is love, the Christian is conformed to him. Christians are full of love to neighbor; full of universal love, not confined to one denomination, not confined to those who agree with his or her opinions or in worship styles, or to those bonded to relatives or those who live nearby. Neither does the Christian love those only who love him or her, or who are intimate friends. But love is like God whose mercy covers all his creation. It soars above all mere boundaries, embracing neighbors and strangers, friends and enemies; yes, not only the good and kind but also the stubbornly wayward and the ungrateful. The Christian loves every person God made, each child from any place or nation. Yet this universal benevolence does not interfere in any way with the special regard for relatives, friends, and helpers; nor does it interfere with a fervent love for country, or endearing affection to all persons of integrity, persons clearly generous and virtuous.

—John Wesley, "A Plain Account of Genuine Christianity," 1753

SELFLESS LOVE

Love of persons, including all humankind, is generous and selfless, springing from no view of advantage to oneself, from no regard to profit or praise, not even the pleasure of loving. This is the daughter, not the parent, of one's affection. By experience one knows that social love—love of neighbor—is absolutely, essentially different from self-love, even of the most allowable kind; but under discipline, each will give additional force to the other until they mix together never to be divided.

—John Wesley, "A Plain Account
of Genuine Christianity," 1753

LOVE RELATES TO OTHERS

This universal selfless love is productive of all right affections. Love produces gentleness, tenderness, sweetness, and courtesy. Love makes a Christian rejoice in the virtues of all, and have a part in their happiness at the same time that he or she sympathizes with their pains and shows compassion for their infirmities. Love creates modesty, fondness, wisdom—together with calmness and evenness of temper. Love is the parent of generosity, openness, and frankness, void of jealousy and suspicion. Love gives birth to candor and willingness to believe and hope whatever is kind and friendly to everyone; and invincible patience, never overcome of evil, but overcoming evil with good.

—John Wesley, "A Plain Account
of Genuine Christianity," 1753

LOVE GOVERNS CONVERSATION

Love constrains Christians to talk not only with strict regard for the truth, but with artless sincerity and genuine simplicity, like one in whom there is no guile. And not content with abstaining from all such expressions contrary to justice and truth, Christians endeavor to refrain from every unloving word, either to people present or about people absent. In all conversation, Christians aim at either improving oneself in knowledge or virtue, or to make those with whom he or she converses in some way wiser, better, or happier than they were before.

—John Wesley, "A Plain Account of Genuine Christianity," 1753

SOCIAL LOVE

ove produces right actions. It leads one into an earnest and steady discharge of all social obligations to relatives, friends, country, and one's own community. Love does not willingly hurt or grieve anyone. It guides one into the consistent practice of justice and mercy. . . . Love impels one to do all possible good, of every possible kind, to all people; and makes one invariably resolved in every circumstance of life to do that, and that only, to others . . . what we expect people to do to us.

—John Wesley, "A Plain Account of Genuine Christianity," 1753

JOHN WESLEY HELPS
A POOR MAN

Here in London a man called on me who had been cheated out of a large fortune and now didn't even have enough to eat. I wanted to put clothes on him and send him back to his home, but I was short of money. However, I asked him to come back in an hour. He did. But before he came, one from whom I expected nothing less, put twenty guineas into my hand. So when the poor fellow returned, I ordered clothing for him from his head to his feet, and sent him straight back to Dublin.

—John Wesley's *Journal*, February 5, 1766

EVERLASTING GOD,
COME DOWN!

es, Amen! let all adore you,
　　High on your eternal throne;
Savior, take the power and glory,
　　Claim the kingdom for your own;
Yes, Jehovah,
　　Everlasting God, come down!

—Charles Wesley, *Intercession Hymns,* 1758

Week Eight

God can put me to what he will,
rank me with whom he will,
put me to doing or to suffering,
employed for God or laid aside for
him, exalted for him or trodden
under foot for him.

Christ will have no servants
except by consent. His people are a
willing people. He will be all in all,
or he will be nothing.

John Wesley

THREE SOURCES OF RENEWAL

𝕴 went to the Bristol cathedral to hear Mr. Handel's *Messiah*. I doubt if that congregation was ever so serious at a sermon as they were during this performance. In many parts, especially several of the choruses, it exceeded my expectation.

I rode to Canterbury. As we came into the city, a stone flew out of the pavement and struck my mare on the leg with such violence that she dropped down at once. I kept my seat till, in struggling to arise, she fell again and rolled over me. When she rose I endeavored to rise too but found I had no use of my right leg or thigh. But an honest barber came out, lifted me up, and helped me into his shop. Feeling myself very sick, I desired a glass of cold water, which instantly gave me ease.

I rode on through an extremely pleasant and fruitful country, to Colchester. I have seen very few such towns in England. It lies on the ridge of a hill, with other hills on each side which run parallel with it at a small distance.

—John Wesley's *Journal*, August 17, October 16 & 27, 1758

BEAUTY, INSPIRATION, PERSPECTIVE

We went to St. Peter's Church, Norwich, to take the Lord's Supper. I scarcely ever remember to have seen a more beautiful parish church; its beauty results not from strange ornaments, but from the very form and structure of it. It is very large and of uncommon height, the sides almost all window. The result: an extraordinary reverential and venerable appearance, yet at the same time, surprisingly cheerful.

Wanting to step into the little church behind the Mansion House, the church commonly called St. Stephen's (Walbrook) in London, I found nothing grand, but a neat and elegant structure beyond expression. I'm not surprised at the speech of the famous Italian architect who met Lord Burlington in Italy: "My Lord, go back and see St. Stephen's in London. We have not so fine a piece of architecture in Rome."

Today I walked all over the famous castle at Colchester, perhaps the most ancient building in England. A considerable part of it, without question, dates back fourteen or fifteen hundred years. It was mostly built with Roman bricks, each of which is about two inches thick, seven broad, and thirteen or fourteen long. Seat of ancient kings, British and Roman, once dreaded far and near! But what are they now? Is not "a living dog better than a dead lion"? And what is it wherein they prided themselves, as if the present great ones of the earth?

A little pomp, a little sway,
    A sunbeam in a winter's day

Is all the great and mighty have
    Between the cradle and the grave!

On Sunday I received much comfort at the old
church in Liverpool in the morning and at St. Thomas's
in the afternoon. It was as if both the sermons had been
made for me. I pity those who can find no good at
church. But how should they if prejudice rears its ugly
head, an effective bar against the grace of God?

—John Wesley's *Journal,* Nov. 5, Dec. 4, 29,
1758 and May 6, 1759

RECOVERY

I preached at Skinner's Alley at five, on Oxmantown Green at eight. My body got weak, but I revived when I saw the seriousness and earnestness of the congregation. I resolved to take advantage of the opportunity and told the people I would preach again in the afternoon; I did and found the congregation much bigger and just as attentive.

When I could, I was only too glad to lie down because I had a fever. However, when the people got together, I got up and went to the meeting. I spoke without pain for nearly an hour. We rejoiced together, knowing God would order all things well.

The next day my fever had increased quite a bit, so I stayed in bed and drank apple juice. On Tuesday I had recovered and wanted to preach, but the doctor insisted that I keep resting. I had planned to ride into the country on Thursday, but the people told me I better not because of the heavy rains. I insisted on keeping my word if possible. One man said his horse could not go out on such a day. But I sent for another horse and at about six rode off, arriving in Killcock about nine.

Between one and two we arrived at Kinnegad. My strength now pretty well gone, I rested an hour, then mounted again, having barely enough energy to sit on my horse. We got along pretty well the next fourteen miles, in about three hours, and by six reached Tyrrel's Pass. At seven I recovered enough to preach and meet the people; they hadn't grown much in numbers, but had in grace.

—John Wesley's *Journal*, April 24, 25 & 28, 1748

THE LOVE OF GOD LIVED
IN THEIR HEARTS

The next day I awakened between three and four
to the sound of a large company of tinners who, fearing
they would miss hearing me, gathered around the house
to sing and praise God. At five I preached once more on,
"Believe on the Lord Jesus Christ, and you will be
saved." They all devoured the Word. Oh, may that Word
give them health for their souls and marrow for strong
bones!

The next day we rode through a village called Stick-
lepath; there someone stopped me in the street and
asked abruptly, "Is not your name John Wesley?" Immediately two or three more came to me to say I must stop
there. I did and before we had spoken many words, our
spirits connected. I found that the people were Quakers.
But they didn't do me harm, for the love of God lived in
their hearts.

—John Wesley's *Journal*, September 21, 1743

STARTING AND GROWING

met a group of soldiers, eight of whom were Scottish Highlanders. Most had a good upbringing but evil communications had corrupted good manners. They all said that from the time they entered the army, they had grown worse and worse. But God had now given them another call, and they knew it.

The more I talk with another group, the more I stand amazed. That God did a great work among them, no one can deny; yet, most of them, believers and unbelievers, cannot give a rational account of the plainest principles of religion. Clearly, God begins his work in the heart; but then he inspires them at high levels to come to understanding.

—John Wesley's *Journal,* May 17 and 22, 1749

DEATH, PREACHING,
AND MARRIAGE

bout noon we came to Aberdare, just as the bell rang for a burial. The funeral brought a great number of people together; after the burial, I preached in the church.

We had had almost continual rain from Aberdare to the great mountain that hangs over the valley of Brecknock, but as soon as we got to the top of the mountain, we left the clouds behind. We had a mild, fair, even sunshiny evening the remainder of the journey.

On Saturday I married my brother to Sarah Gwynne. What a solemn day! A day to show the dignity of Christian marriage.

—John Wesley's *Journal,* April 6 and 7, 1749

FIELD PREACHING

J marvel at those who still talk so loudly about the indecency of field preaching. The highest indecency surfaces in St. Paul's Church, when a considerable part of the congregation fall asleep, or talk, or look about, not paying attention to a word the preacher says. On the other hand, the highest decency takes place in a church-yard or field when the whole congregation behave and look as if they saw the Judge of all and heard him speak from heaven.

—John Wesley's *Journal*, August 28, 1748

Week Nine

A violent hail storm came up. I tried to get the people to cover their heads; most of them would not, and no one went away until I finished preaching.

John Wesley

THE POWER OF PREACHING

I rode to Clara, where I learned that in an hour's time a famous cockfight would take place, to which almost all the people in the areas would come. Hoping to engage part of the group in something better, I began preaching in the street as soon as I could. One of two hundred stopped, listened awhile, took off their hats, and forgot about the cockfight.

The congregation at Tullamore in the evening proved larger than ever, and deep attention sat on every face. Toward the end of the sermon, a violent hail storm came up. I tried to get the people to cover their heads; most of them would not, and no one went away until I finished preaching.

—John Wesley's *Journal*, April 12, 1748

THE SCILLY ISLES

I had for some time a great desire to go tell the
love of God our Savior, even for one day, in the Isles of
Scilly. I had occasionally mentioned this to several.

This evening, three men offered to take me if I could
borrow the mayor's boat, the best in town. The mayor
agreed immediately. So the next morning, Tuesday the
13th, John Nelson, Mr. Sheppard and I, with three men
and a pilot, sailed from St. Ives. I felt strange sailing in a
fishing boat on the ocean, especially when the waves
began to swell and hang over our heads. But I asked my
companions to sing with me; we sang lustily and with
good courage:

> When passing through the watery deep,
>   I ask in faith his promised aid;
> The waves an awful distance keep,
>   And shrink from my devoted head;
> Fearless their violence I dare:
>   they cannot harm — for God is there.

About 1:30 we landed on St. Mary's, the chief of the
inhabited islands.

Immediately we went to the governor, with the usual
present, a newspaper. I preached in the streets at six;
almost the whole town, with many soldiers, sailors and
workmen, came to listen to my sermon on, "Why will
you die, O house of Israel?" We had such a blessed time I
hardly knew how to conclude. After the sermon, I gave
the people little books and hymns, which they received
with such eagerness they seemed ready to tear both
them and me to pieces.

At five in the morning I preached on, "I will heal their backslidings; I will love them freely." Between nine and ten, I talked to my people privately, then distributed between two and three hundred hymns and small books.

—John Wesley's *Journal*, September 12, 1743

PREACHING IN SPITE OF...

After preaching at Oakhill about noon, I rode to Shepton and found the people strangely upset. A mob, they said, hired, prepared, and made drunk enough to hurt us, aimed to do a lot of damage. I began preaching somewhere between four and five o'clock, but no one hindered or interrupted at all. God blessed us with a real opportunity to preach, and the hearts of many got a great deal of comfort. I wondered what had become of the mob. But we got quick information: they mistook the place, supposing I would have dismounted, as I used to, at William Stone's house, and had summoned, by drum, all their forces to meet me when I arrive. But Mr. Swindells innocently took me to the other end of town. They did not discover their mistake until I had stopped preaching. They had in fact, designed to stop my preaching, but suffered complete disappointment!

However they followed us from the place where I preached as we rode to William Stone's, throwing dirt, stones, and lots of clods. But they could not hurt us. Mr. Swindells got a little dirt on his coat, and I a few specks on my hat.

—John Wesley's *Journal,* February 12, 1748

GOD, HIDDEN SOURCE
OF CALM REPOSE

God, hidden source of calm repose,
You, all-sufficient love divine,
My help and refuge from my foes,
Secure I am, if you are mine:
And lo! from sin, and grief, and shame,
I hide me, Jesus, in your name.

Your mighty name salvation is,
And keeps my happy soul above;
Comfort it brings, and power, and peace,
And joy, and everlasting love:
To me with your dear name are given
Pardon, and holiness, and heaven.

Jesus, my all in all you are,
My rest in toil, my ease in pain;
The med'cine of my broken heart,
In war my peace, in loss my gain;
My smile beneath the tyrant's frown,
In shame my glory and my crown.

In want my plentiful supply,
In weakness my almighty power;
In bonds my perfect liberty,
My light in satan's darkest hour;
In grief my joy unspeakable,
My life in death, my heaven in hell.

—Charles Wesley, *Hymns and Sacred Poems,* 1742

PREACHING AND
BEHAVIOR CHANGE

rode, at the suggestion of John Bennet, to Rochdale in Lancashire. As soon as we entered the town, we found the streets lined on both sides with crowds of people shouting, cursing, blaspheming, and acting in a terrible way. Sensing the impracticality of preaching on the streets, I went into a large room, open to the street, and called loudly, "Let the wicked forsake their ways, and the unrighteous people their thoughts." The Word of God prevailed over the fierceness of people. No one opposed or interrupted; more, we could see remarkable change in the behavior of the people as we later left the town.

—John Wesley's *Journal*, October 18, 1749

COVERED FROM END TO END

At Trezuthan Down, I preached to two or three thousand people on the "highway" of the Lord, the way of holiness. We reached Gwennap a little before six and found the meadow covered from end to end. I suppose I preached to 10,000 about Christ our "wisdom, righteousness, sanctification, and redemption." I could not stop preaching until it got so dark we could hardly see one another. Everyone gave the deepest attention, no one speaking, stirring, or scarcely looking aside. Surely here, though in a temple not made with hands, we worshiped God in "the beauty of holiness."

—John Wesley's *Journal*, September 20, 1743

DIVINE PROTECTION

By gentle degrees, God prepares us for his will!
Two years ago, a piece of brick grazed my shoulder. A
year after that, a stone struck me between the eyes. Last
month, I received a blow, and this evening two, one
before we came into town, and one after we got into
town. But they didn't phase me, though one man struck
me in the chest with all his might, and the other on the
mouth with such force the blood gushed out immediately; I felt no more pain from either than if the men had
touched me with a straw.

Most of the people made all haste to escape for their
lives, but four would not stir, William Sitch, Edward
Slater, John Griffiths, and Joan Parks. These stayed with
me, resolving to live or die together. Only William Sitch
received a blow, but he held me by the arm from one end
of town to the other. Dragged away and knocked down,
William soon got up and returned to me. Later I asked
him what he thought. He answered, "To die for Christ
who had died for us." He said he had no fear or hurry,
but calmly waited for God to take him to heaven.

I asked Joan Parks if she suffered fear when the men
tore her away from me. She said, "No, no more than I
have now. I could trust God for you, as well as for myself. From the beginning, God fully persuaded me he
would deliver you. I did not know how, but I left that to
him, and felt as sure as if he had already done it." I asked
her about a report that she had fought for me. She said,
"No; I knew God would fight for his children."

Later I found Christian people praying, many of
whom I had never seen. The next morning, as I rode

through the town on my way to Nottingham, everyone I met expressed such a cordial affection that I could scarcely believe what I saw and heard.

—John Wesley's *Journal*, October 20, 1743

Week Ten

O grant that nothing in my soul
   May dwell, but *thy pure love alone!*
O may thy *love possess me whole,*
   My joy, my treasure, and my crown;
Strange fires far from my heart remove:
   My *every act, word, thought be love!*

John Wesley's translation of
a hymn by Paul Gerhardt

OH, FOR A HEART
TO PRAISE MY GOD

for a heart to praise my God,
A heart from sin set free!
A heart that always feels your blood,
So freely spilt for me!

A heart resigned, submissive, meek,
My great Redeemer's throne,
Where only Christ is heard to speak,
Where Jesus reigns alone.

A heart in every thought renewed,
And full of love divine,
Perfect, and right, and pure, and good—
A copy, Lord, of thine!

Your nature, gracious Lord, impart;
Come quickly from above;
Write your new name upon my heart,
Your new, best name of love!

—Charles Wesley, *Hymns & Sacred Poems*, 1742

PURE INTENTIONS

In the year 1725, my twenty-third year, I discovered Bishop Taylor's *Rules and Exercises of Holy Living and Dying.* Several parts of this book got under my skin, especially the part that refers to *pure intentions.* At once I decided to dedicate *all my life* to God, all my thoughts and words and actions. I saw no half-way house; Taylor convinced me thoroughly that *every part* of my life (not just part of it!) I must either give to God or to myself. And if to myself, that would mean giving myself to the devil!

Now then, can any thoughtful person doubt this road to pure intentions? Can anyone really find a compromise between serving God or the devil?

—John Wesley, *A Plain Account of Christian Perfection,* 1766

"THE WINGS OF THE SOUL"

In the year 1726, I discovered Thomas à Kempis'
Imitation of Christ. The nature and extent of inward
religion, the religion of the heart, got to me as it never
had. I saw I must give up all my life to God (assuming
this possible), but that in itself would profit nothing
unless I *gave my heart;* yes! *all my heart* to him. I saw that
"simplicity of intention and pure love"—*one grand design*
behind all we say and do—and *one desire* ruling all our
emotions—that design and desire become "the wings of
the soul" without which our spirits can never fly to God.

—John Wesley, *A Plain Account of Christian Perfection,* 1766

HALF A CHRISTIAN

year or two after, Mr. Law's *Christian Perfection*, and *Serious Call* came to my attention. These convinced me more than ever of the absolute impossibility of being *half a Christian*. And I determined through his grace (I sensed deeply the absolute necessity of grace) to live *all-devoted* to God, to give him *all* my soul, my body, and my substance.

Can any thoughtful person say that I carried matters *too far?* Or that anything *less* could pass muster with him who has given himself for us? Surely, then, we must give ourselves to him. Yes, *all* we have, and *all* we are.

—John Wesley, *A Plain Account of Christian Perfection,* 1766

MY ULTIMATE AUTHORITY

In the year 1729, I began the serious *study* of the Bible. I saw the Bible as the one and only standard of truth, the only model of pure religion. So, in clearer and clearer light, I perceived the indispensable necessity of having *the mind that was in Christ,* and *walking as Christ also walked.* I realized that Christ could not have just *some part* of my mind, but all of it, that I must walk as he walked, not only in *many* or *most* respects, but in *all* things.

So this light made vivid my perception of religion. I must follow Christ just *one way: entire* conformity, inward and outward, to our Master. I feared nothing except *bending* this rule to my own or others' experience. To bend the rule would mean disconformity to our great Example.

—John Wesley, *A Plain Account of Christian Perfection,* 1766

THE CIRCUMCISION
OF THE HEART

On January 1, 1733, I preached before the University of Oxford (in St. Mary's Church) on "The Circumcision of the Heart." I defined circumcision as that habit of the soul, called holiness in spiritual literature, that directly implies cleansing from sin, from all filth of flesh and spirit, which results in the goodness Christ Jesus had; in other words, a renewed image of the mind that makes our heavenly Father look at us as perfect.

In that same sermon, I observed that love fulfills the law, that love is the purpose of God's commands. Love is not only the first and last commandment, it wraps up all the commandments into one. "Whatever is just, whatever is pure, whatever is good, whatever comes from praise"—they all comprise one word, love. Love brings perfection, honor and happiness. The royal law of heaven and earth? Love the Lord your God with all your heart, soul, mind, strength. Herein lies your ultimate purpose in life.

I concluded that sermon by saying that *the perfect law* is the circumcision of the heart. God will not compromise on that point. When we refuse to think, speak or act to fulfill our own will, but only his will, whether we eat or drink, or whatever we do, then we do all to God's glory.

Can anyone who knows the Bible deny that the Bible teaches just this?

—John Wesley, *A Plain Account of Christian Perfection*, 1766

REIGN ALONE!

When I stayed in Savannah, in America, I wrote these lines:

> Is there a thing beneath the sun
>> That strives with thee my heart to share?
> Ah tear it thence, and *reign alone*,
>> The Lord of *every motion* there!

At the beginning of the year 1738, returning from America, the cry of my heart issued in the these lines:

> O Grant that nothing in my soul
>> May dwell, but *thy pure love alone!*
> O may thy *love possess me whole*,
>> My joy, my treasure, and my crown;
> Strange fires far from my heart remove:
>> My *every act, word, thought be love!*

I never heard anyone object to this; indeed, who can? Surely believers, every one of them, use this kind of language, at least everyone truly awakened. I have never written anything stronger than these lines of poetry.

—John Wesley, *A Plain Account of Christian Perfection,* 1766

Week Eleven

Beware of singing as if you
were half dead or half asleep; but
lift up your voice with strength.

Above all sing spiritually. Have an
eye to God in every word you sing.
Aim at pleasing him more than
yourself or any other creature.

John Wesley

DIRECTIONS FOR SINGING

I. Learn these tunes before you learn any others; afterwards learn as many as you please.

II. Sing them exactly as they are printed here, without altering or mending them at all; and if you have learned to sing them otherwise, unlearn it as soon as you can.

III. Sing all. See that you join with the congregation as frequently as you can. Let not a slight degree of weakness or weariness hinder you. If it is a cross to you, take it up, and you will find it a blessing.

IV. Sing lustily and with a good courage. Beware of singing as if you were half dead or half asleep; but lift up your voice with strength. Be no more afraid of your voice now nor more ashamed of its being heard than when you sang the songs of Satan.

V. Sing modestly. Do not bawl, so as to be heard above or distinct from the rest of the congregation, that you may not destroy the harmony; but strive to unite your voices together so as to make one clear melodious sound.

VI. Sing in time. Whatever time is sung be sure to keep with it. Do not run before nor stay behind it; but attend close to the leading voices, and more therewith as exactly as you can; and take care not to sing too slowly. This drawling way naturally steals on all who are lazy; and it is high time to drive it out from us, and sing all our tunes just as quickly as we did at first.

VII. Above all sing spiritually. Have an eye to God in every word you sing. Aim at pleasing him more than yourself or any other creature. In order to do this attend strictly to the sense of what you sing, and see that your heart is not carried away with the sound, but offered to God continually; so shall your singing be such as the Lord will approve here, and reward you when he comes in the clouds of heaven.

—John Wesley, from the Preface to *Sacred Melody*, 1761

OH, FOR A THOUSAND TONGUES TO SING

O for a thousand tongues to sing
My dear Redeemer's praise!
The glories of my God and King,
The triumphs of his grace!

My gracious Master, and my God,
Assist me to proclaim,
To spread through all the earth abroad
The honor of thy name.

Jesus, the name that charms our fears,
That bids our sorrows cease—
'Tis music in the sinner's ears,
'Tis life, and health, and peace.

He breaks the power of cancelled sin,
He sets the prisoner free;
His blood can make the foulest clean—
His blood availed for me.

He speaks, and listening to his voice
New life the dead receive;
The mournful, broken hearts rejoice,
The humble poor believe.

Hear him, ye deaf; his praise, ye dumb,
Your loosened tongues employ;
Ye blind, behold your Savior come,
And leap, ye lame, for joy!

Look unto him, ye nations, own
Your God, ye fallen race;

Look, and be saved through faith alone,
Be justified by grace.

See all your sins on Jesus laid:
The Lamb of God was slain,
His soul was once an offering made
For every soul of man.

—Charles Wesley on the anniversary of his conversion, 1739

SINGING IN THE SPIRIT

At five I had the pleasure of hearing the whole congregation "sing with the spirit and the understanding also". . . .

At six I preached and could not but observe such singing as I have seldom heard in England. The women, in particular, sang so exactly that it seemed but one voice.

I went on to Edinburgh where I heard surprisingly good singing in the evening. I have not heard such female voices, so strong and clear, anywhere in England.

We went to church a little before twelve, where the singing was admirably good. The clerk teaches them to sing.

—John Wesley's *Journal*, August 10, 1768; April 30, 1775;
May 27, 1779; June 7, 1789.

MORNING HYMN

Christ, whose glory fills the skies,
Christ, the true, the only Light,
Sun of righteousness, arise,
Triumph o'er the shade of night;
Day-spring from on high, be near;
Day-star, in my heart appear!

Dark and cheerless is the morn,
Unaccompanied by thee:
Joyless is the day's return,
Till thy mercy's beams I see:
Till thou inward light impart,
Glad my eyes, and warm my heart.

Visit then this soul of mine,
Pierce the gloom of sin and grief;
Fill me, Radiancy Divine!
Scatter all my unbelief:
More and more thyself display,
Shining to the perfect day!

—John Wesley, *Hymns and Spiritual Poems I*, 1740

MUSIC AND ANIMALS

I thought it worthwhile to make an odd experiment. Remembering how surprisingly fond of music the lion at Edinburgh was, I decided to see if animals similar to lions responded to music, too. So I went to the Tower of London with one who plays the German flute. He began playing close to four or five lions; one of the four got up, came to the front of his den, and seemed to be all attention. In the meantime, a tiger in the same den got up, leaped over the lion's back, turned and ran under his belly, leaped over him again, and so he went back and forth, non-stop. How do we account for this?

I rode to Coolalough to a Quarterly Meeting, and preached at eleven as well as in the evening. While we sang, I noted with surprise that the horses from all parts of the ground gathered about us. Is it true then that horses, as well as lions and tigers, have an ear for music?

—John Wesley's *Journal*, December 31, 1764; July 3, 1769

CHILDREN SINGING

About three, I met between nine hundred and a thousand children from our Sunday schools. I never saw such a sight. Clean and plain in dress, they came in a serious mood and behaved well. Both boys and girls had as beautiful faces as one could see in England or Europe. When they all sang together, none of them out of tune, the melody soared beyond what one could hear in a theater; best of all, many really believe God and some know true salvation. These children model for the whole town. They visit the poor and sick, sometimes six or eight, even ten children together, to encourage, comfort and pray by themselves; sometimes even 30 or 40 do this. They become so absorbed in singing, praying and crying, they don't want to part. "Out of the mouths of babes and infants. . . ."

—John Wesley's *Journal*, April 20, 1788

ANTHEMS

At nine I explained the great text of St. John to an exceedingly large congregation. We had an anthem which I never heard these 50 years, "Praise the Lord, O My Soul." The choir sang in a manner that would not have disgraced any of our English cathedrals.

In the evening I preached at Pebworth church; but I seemed out of my element. A long anthem was sung; but I suppose none beside the singers could understand one word of it.

I came just in time to put a stop to a bad custom creeping in here; a few men, who had fine voices, sang a psalm which no one knew, in a tune fit for an opera, with three, four or five persons singing different words at the same time! What an insult on common sense! What a burlesque on public worship! No custom can excuse such a mixture of profaneness and absurdity.

About six we went to church, pretty well filled with people we did not expect to see so near the Highlands. But we were much more surprised at their singing. Thirty or 40 sang an anthem after the sermon; they sang in such good voice and fine judgment that I doubt any cathedral in England could excel them.

—John Wesley's *Journal,* June 6, 1773; March 19, 1778; April 8, 1781; May 7, 1761

Week Twelve

J believe Jesus of Nazareth is
the world's Savior. . . .

He will reign until the whole
world knows he is King.

John Wesley

WHO IS JESUS CHRIST?

At just the right time in history, God sent his only Son into the world; a woman gave birth to him, and God watched over her. God announced his Son's coming to shepherds, to a devout man called Simeon, to Anna the prophetess, and to everyone who waited in Jerusalem for God to redeem the world.

When old enough to do the job God sent him to do, Israel heard about him, and he preached the gospel of the kingdom of God in every town and in every city. For a while everyone thought well of him; everybody said he spoke very differently from any other person, that he preached and taught with authority, and with all the wisdom and power of God. God documented the authenticity of Jesus by signs and wonders and mighty works that Jesus did, as well as by his whole life. He never sinned at any time in his life, and everything he did he did well. He did nothing selfishly but did only the will of God who sent him.

—John Wesley's sermon, "The End of Christ's Coming," 1788

"I BELIEVE"

believe Jesus of Nazareth is the world's Savior, the Messiah foretold a long time before he came, the One anointed with the Holy Spirit and therefore a prophet, revealing to us the whole will of God. A priest, who gave himself as a sacrifice for sin, he still makes intercession for sinners. A king, with all power in heaven and earth, he will reign until the whole world knows he is King.

I believe he is the real and natural Son of God, God himself, and Lord of all, with absolute, supreme and universal authority over all things. But I believe that more especially, he is our Lord—i.e., for those who believe in him.

I believe he always existed. Jesus, human nature and the divine nature living in one person conceived by the Holy Spirit, was born of the blessed Virgin Mary.

I believe he suffered inexpressible pains in both body and soul, then died on a cross when Pontius Pilate governed Judea under the Roman Emperor. While his body lay in the grave, his soul went to the place of departed spirits. On the third day he rose from the dead. Then he ascended to heaven where he remains on the throne in highest power and honor as Mediator, until the end of the world. He will come in the end times from heaven to judge everyone of us about our work, both those who have already died and those still alive.

—John Wesley, Letter to a Roman Catholic, July 18, 1749

THE FOUNDATION
OF ALL OUR HOPE

bout noon I preached at Warrington, but not to the taste of some of my hearers, I'm afraid. My subject led me to speak strongly and explicitly about God in Christ. But that I cannot help, because on this I *must* insist as foundation of all our hope.

—John Wesley's *Journal*, April 5, 1768

JESUS, THE NAME
HIGH OVER ALL

Jesus, the name high over all
In hell, or earth, or sky;
Angels and men before it fall,
And devils fear and fly.

Jesus, the name to sinners dear,
The name to sinners given.
It scatters all their guilty fear,
It turns their hell to heaven.

Jesus the prisoner's fetters breaks,
And bruises Satan's head,
Power into strengthless souls it speaks,
And life into the dead.

O that the world might taste and see
The riches of his grace!
The arms of love that compass me
Would all mankind embrace.

O that my Jesu's heavenly charms
Might every bosom move!
Fly, sinners, fly into those arms
Of everlasting love.

His only righteousness I show,
His saving truth proclaim:
'Tis all my business here below,
To cry, "Behold the Lamb!"

Happy, if with my latest breath
I may but gasp his name!
Preach him to all, and cry in death,
"Behold! behold the Lamb."

—Charles Wesley in *Hymns and Sacred Poems,* 1749

WHAT CHRIST DOES

The Son of God strikes at the root of that grand work of the devil—pride. He causes the sinner to humble him or herself before the Lord. He strikes at the root of self-will, enabling the humbled sinner to say, "Not my will but his." Christ destroys the love of the world, delivering those who believe in him from "every foolish and hurtful desire," from the "desire of the flesh, the desire of the eyes, and the pride of life." Christ saves believers from seeking or expecting happiness in any creature. As Satan turned the heart from the Creator to the creature, so the Son of God turns the heart back again from the creature to the Creator. So by manifesting himself, he destroys the works of the devil, restoring the guilty outcast to God's favor, and to pardon and peace; restoring the sinner in whom there is no good, to love and holiness; delivering the burdened, miserable sinner to joy beyond description, and to real, meaningful happiness.

—John Wesley's sermon, "The End of Christ's Coming," 1781

CHRIST OUR MEDIATOR

There is one God and those who do not have him through the one Mediator do not have God. We could not rejoice that there is a God if we did not have a Mediator, one who stands between God and us to reconcile us to God and to transact this whole affair called salvation. This excludes all other mediators, like saints and angels and idols. Heathen peoples, a long time ago, set up many mediators to pacify their gods.

—John Wesley, *Explanatory notes Upon The New Testament*, 1754

JESUS, MY LORD

Jesus, my Lord, attend
Your fallen creature's cry
And show yourself the sinner's Friend,
And set me up on high:
From hell's oppressive power,
From earth and sin release,
And to the Father's grace restore,
And to your perfect peace.

For this, alas! I mourn
In helpless unbelief,
But you my wretched heart can turn,
And heal my sin and grief;
Salvation in your name
To dying souls is given,
And all may, through your merit, claim
A right to life and heaven.

—Charles Wesley, *Poetics*, 1774

Week Thirteen

You will have a double blessing if you give yourself up to the Great Physician so he may heal soul and body together.

John Wesley

HEALING AND SPIRITUAL FORMATION

If the return of your disorder lessens more and more, you have reason to hope that, at length, you will experience total healing. Very probably, if you live to 25 or 26, your body will take a new turn. But certainly the design of God, who loves you, is to heal both body and soul, and possibly he delays the healing of the former so that the cure of the latter will keep pace with it.

—John Wesley, *Letters*, to Alexander Knox, March 19, 1777

JOHN WESLEY'S CONCERN
FOR A YOUNG GIRL

My Dear Betsy:

I hope you have not fallen ill again. Tell me about your health and your mental state. Do you stay close, consistently, to God? Are you always happy? Do you allow circumstances to interrupt or deaden your spirit of prayer? Do you always surrender to God? Can you sing this hymn with your whole heart?

> Determined all thy will to obey,
>   Thy blessings I restore;
> Give, Lord, or take thy gifts away,
>   I praise Thee evermore.

—John Wesley, *Letters*, to Elizabeth Ritchie, July 15, 1776

THE LONG-TERM VALUE OF CONSISTENT EXERCISE

Air and exercise you must have; and if you use constant exercise with an exact regimen, not improbably you will have vigorous health if you live to 34 or 35. About that time the constitution, both of men and women, frequently takes an entire turn.

—John Wesley, *Letters*, to Miss March, June 17, 1774

BELIEVE AND RECEIVE

irection as to this or that way is as much an answer to prayer as if the cure took place immediately. But you will have a double blessing if you give yourself up to the Great Physician so he may heal soul and body together. And unquestionably this is his design. He wants to give you and my dear Mrs. Knox both inward and outward health. And why not now? Surely he stands ready: believe and receive the blessing.

Doubtlessly your bodily disorder greatly affects your mind. Exercise care in preventing the disease by diet rather than by medicine. Look up, and wait for happy days!

—John Wesley, *Letters,* to Alexander Knox, October 26, 1778

GIVE GOD ALL CREDIT

Wisdom does not tell us to credit health or any other blessing merely to natural causes. Ascribe all to him whose kingdom rules over all. More, whether we have more or less bodily strength does not compare to living strong in the Lord and in the power of his might. He gives strength when needed.

—John Wesley, *Letters*, to his sister Mrs. Hall, June 3, 1776

GOD'S BEST

Your present illness will, I hope, prove a real blessing. You suffered the danger of having more sail than ballast, more liveliness of imagination than solid wisdom. But God, correcting this defect, now gives you more steadiness of mind. You now see and feel the real worth of this poor, perishable world, and how little actual happiness one can find in all things under the sun.

—John Wesley, *Letters,* to Philothea Briggs,
September 13, 1771

A SECRET TO LONG LIFE
AND GOOD HEALTH

The lengthening of your life and the restoring of your health are invaluable blessings. But do you ask how you can improve them to the glory of the Giver? And do you really want to know? Then I will tell you now.

Go see the poor and sick in their own poor little hovels. Take up your cross, woman. Remember the faith! Jesus went before you, and will go with you. Put off the gentlewoman; you bear a higher character.

—John Wesley, *Letters,* to Miss March, June 9, 1775

Week Fourteen

🍂

I cannot advise you in the meantime to shut yourself up at home; that is neither good for your body nor your mind. You cannot possibly have bodily health without daily exercise in the open air; and you have no reason to expect the spirit of a healthful mind unless you use the means that God has ordained.

John Wesley

GOD'S HEALING GRACE

On the 17th of last June, I finished my eightieth year. When young, I had weak eyes, trembling hands, and all kinds of physical hang-ups. But, by the blessing of God, I have outlived them all! I have no physical problems now except what naturally accompany flesh and blood. Look what God has done for me!

You lack the grand medicine I use: exercise and change of air.

—John Wesley, *Letters*, to Walter Sellon, January 10, 1784

SOME RULES FOR MAINTAINING GOOD HEALTH

1. Everyone who wants to preserve good health, must maintain clean, sweet-smelling houses, clothes and furniture.

2. The great rule of eating and drinking: control the quality and quantity of food to the ability of your digestive system; always take the kind of food and the measure of food that sits lightly and easily on your stomach.

3. The right amount of exercise is indispensably necessary to health and long life.

4. People without strong constitutions need to go to bed early and get up early.

—John Wesley, *Primitive Physic: An Easy and Natural Method of Curing Most Diseases*, first edition, 1747; 23d edition, 1791

RULES FOR EXERCISING

1. Walking is the best exercise for those able to do it; horseback riding for those not able. Open air contributes a great deal to the benefits of exercise.

2. We can strengthen any weak part of the body by consistent exercise. For example, strengthen your lungs by projective speaking, or by walking up an easy hill. Help digestion and the nervous system by horse riding. One more example: make your arms and upper legs stronger by daily massage.

3. People who do a lot of sitting in their work, need to schedule times for exercise, at least two or three hours a day: half of this before a big noon meal, the other half before going to bed.

4. Those who read and write a great deal, should learn to do their work while standing; otherwise, their health will suffer.

5. Do not exercise past your fatigue point. Never continue when wearied. After exercise, take care to cool down by degrees.

—John Wesley, Primitive Physic: *An Easy and Natural Method of Curing Most Diseases*, first edition, 1747; 23d edition, 1791

RULES FOR HEALTHFUL EATING

1. Nothing encourages good health more than abstinence, plain food, and hard work.

2. For people who sit at their work, about 8 ounces of animal food and 12 of vegetable, in 24 hours, is sufficient.

3. The best of all drinks is water; it quickens the appetite and strengthens the digestion most.

4. Strong drinks, especially those high in alcohol content, mean certain, though slow, poison.

5. Experience shows little danger in stopping liquor all at once.

6. Coffee and tea hurt people with weak nerves a great deal.

7. People with weak constitutions need to eat only light suppers, and that two or three hours before going to bed.

—John Wesley, *Primitive Physic: An Easy and Natural Method of Curing Most Diseases*, first edition, 1747; 23d edition, 1791

EMOTIONS AND HEALTH

1. Emotions have a greater influence on health than most people realize.

2. All violent or sudden emotions open the door to, or actually throw people into, acute diseases.

3. Slow, lasting emotions, such as grief or hopeless love, bring on chronic diseases.

4. Until the emotion that causes the disease gets calm, medicine will not help.

5. The love of God is the sovereign remedy for all miseries. It effectively prevents bodily disorders the emotions introduce, by keeping emotions within their proper boundaries. And by the unspeakable joy, perfect calm, serenity, and tranquility love gives the mind, it becomes the most powerful of all the means to health and long life.

—John Wesley, *Primitive Physic: An Easy and Natural Method of Curing Most Diseases,* first edition 1747; 23d edition, 1791

THE EXERCISE HORSE

... You should be sure to take as much exercise every day as you can bear. I wish you could borrow George Whitefield's chamber-horse [exercise horse] out of my dining room, which you should use half an hour at least every day.

—John Wesley, *Letters,* to his niece Sarah Wesley,
August 18, 1790

HEALTH AND SPIRITUAL DYNAMICS

In the meantime, see that you neglect no possible means of restoring your health. Send me, from time to time, a specific account of your state of health. Have you given your own *will* totally to God, so you have no resistance to his will in anything? Do you find no stirring of pride? no remains of vanity? no desire of praise or fear of correction? Do you enjoy an uninterrupted sense of the loving presence of God? Do you keep in good spirits no matter the health of your body? Your illness naturally sinks the spirits and brings heaviness and dejection. Can you, nonetheless, "rejoice evermore and in everything give thanks"?

—John Wesley, *Letters*, to Hester Ann Rose, May 3, 1776

Week Fifteen

❧

In the year 1726, I discovered Thomas à Kempis' *Christian's Pattern*. The nature and extent of *inward religion*, the religion of the heart, now appeared to me in a stronger light than ever. I saw that giving *all my life* to God would profit me nothing unless I gave my *heart*, yes *all my heart* to him.

John Wesley

HOW TO READ
THOMAS À KEMPIS

I write out a few plain directions on how to read this (or any other religious book) with an eye to growing spiritually.

1. Assign yourself a specific time each day. If necessary business unexpectedly robs you of your devotional period, take the next hour. We give ourselves a lot of opportunity for eating, why not adequate time for spiritual reading to improve our soul?

2. Prepare yourself for reading by purity of intention, aiming to improve yourself. In a short prayer, ask God's grace to enlighten your understanding and open your heart for receiving what you read, so you can know what God requires of you and then put feet to what he says.

3. Do not read out of mere curiosity or too fast; rather, read unhurriedly, seriously, and with careful attention. Stop now and then to process fresh insights. Pause, too, for remembering what you read and to think through how to apply it. Then, too, don't jump around in your reading, passing from one thing to another—that's like tasting too many dishes without allowing yourself to find satisfaction in any. Read some passages over and again, especially those that deeply concern you yourself; then ponder how to put them into practice.

4. Work at putting yourself in a frame of mind that corresponds with what you read. Otherwise, it will prove empty and unprofitable, while it only enlightens your understanding but fails to influence your

will or set fire to your emotions. Therefore, lift up petitions now and again for God's grace. Also, write out some quotable sayings; treasure them in your memory bank to meditate on so that when temptations come, you have your quiver full of arrows against sins you may be addicted to. These quotable materials will also help you develop humility and patience, increase your love for God, and enrich any other virtue.

5. Conclude your reading time with a short prayer to God, asking him to preserve and prosper the good seed sown in your heart, so it will yield fruit in its season. And don't think these devotional times are wasted; in fact, you could not use your time to better advantage!

—Preface to John Wesley's edition of *The Christian's Pattern*
(or *An Extract of The Imitation of Christ*
by Thomas à Kempis), 1746

IMITATE CHRIST

1. Christ said that if we follow him we won't walk in darkness. Here he tells us to imitate him if we want to live as he did and behave as he did. If we do that, we will know true enlightenment and be delivered from all blindness of heart.

   Therefore, make your chief endeavor to meditate on the life of Jesus Christ.

2. What good will come to you, even if you debate superbly about the Trinity? If you don't live humbly, you will displease the Trinity!

   In actual fact, elevated words do not make one holy or just; only a virtuous life makes one dear to God.

   I would rather *feel* remorse than know its definition.

   If you know the whole Bible and the sayings of all the philosophers by memory, what good will that do you without God's love?

—John Wesley's edition of Thomas à Kempis'
The Christian's Pattern, 1746

VANITY OF VANITIES!
ALL IS VANITY

1. "Vanity of vanities! all is vanity" . . . but to love God and serve him only.

2. Therefore, merely to feed your ego by riches, honors, lust, work that ends up in grief—all that's foolish. It's also foolish only to wish to live a long time while living carelessly instead of well. At the same time, it's foolish to give attention only to this present existence, ignoring the life to come. By the same token, it's vain to focus on what passes away quickly, but to give no notice to everlasting joys.

—John Wesley's edition of Thomas à Kempis'
The Christian's Pattern, 1746

BE CAREFUL ABOUT
WHAT YOU KNOW

1. Normal people want to learn, but knowledge without respect for God amounts to nothing.

   A humble steward who serves God surpasses the proud philosopher who neglects his personal salvation while studying the stars in their courses.

   To know yourself is to know your capacity for doing bad things. So be careful about the praises of human beings!

   If I know everything but don't have love, how could that knowledge help me from the divine Judge's point of view?

2. Don't desire knowledge you shouldn't have, but would send you on an ego trip and divert your attention from important matters.

   You could know a lot that would not help you.

   Unwise people seek knowledge that does not improve their souls.

   Many big words will not bring your spirit to fulfillment, but a pure conscience will give you confidence in God's presence.

3. The more you know and understand, the greater you will be judged unless you live increasingly more holy.

   Therefore, don't get the big head about your learning; rather, use your knowledge to increase your respect for God the All-Knowing One.

   If you think you know a great deal, remember you have much more to learn.

Don't come across as too wise, but acknowledge your ignorance.

If you want to know with profit, love the quiet life where people don't pay much attention to you.

—John Wesley's edition of Thomas à Kempis'
The Christian's Pattern, 1746

SELF-KNOWLEDGE

1. The highest, most profitable lesson is true knowledge of ourselves.

   You possess great wisdom to see yourself modestly and always to view others highly and in a good light.

2. If you see someone in open sin, don't elevate yourself, assuming you have a better nature than the sinner.

   All human beings are frail, but remember, none more frail than yourself.

> —John Wesley's edition of Thomas à Kempis'
> *The Christian's Pattern,* 1746

TRUTH

1. **D**o you want to be happy? Let truth itself teach you. Not by pretty pictures and words that pass away, but by an immediate communication itself.

   Our own opinion and sense often deceive us, and we discern little.

   What help do we really get talking about hidden matters? Being ignorant of obscurities will not militate against us at judgment day.

   But what folly to neglect the profitable and give attention to the merely curious or hurtful things!

2. From the one Word comes all truth; and that Word talks to us. No one can evaluate rightly without him. Here lies the secret of stability and peace.

   O God, the Truth, make me one with you in eternal love. I grow weary of hearing so much; in you I find all I really desire. Let everyone go silent before you; speak alone to me.

3. Who has a sharper battle than the one who labors to overcome self? Our real business: to conquer self, and every day to advance in holy living.

   A humble knowledge of oneself brings us more certainly to God than a deep search for science. Yet knowledge itself God ordained, so it's okay; but a good conscience and a true life always come before learning.

—John Wesley's edition of Thomas à Kempis'
The Christian's Pattern, 1746

WISE ACTION

1. We must not listen to every idea, but evaluate after the pattern of God's will.

   Yet in our weakness we often believe too easily and end up saying something evil, rather than good, of others.

   Good persons do not readily give credit to everything one tells them because they know human frailty leads to evil and tends to fail in the use of words.

2. Great wisdom does not proceed rashly nor stand stiffly on one's own opinion.

   Consult a prudent and conscientious person, seeking instruction by one better than yourself rather than following your own inclinations without accountability.

   A good life makes one wise according to God and provides experience in a wide range of matters.

   The humbler, the more surrendered to God, and therefore the more sensible and contented you will be no matter what your situation.

—John Wesley's edition of Thomas à Kempis'
The Christian's Pattern, 1746

Week Sixteen

Give admittance to Christ and deny entrance to all others.

John Wesley

ABOUT THE INWARD LIFE

The kingdom of God is within you, says the Lord. Turn with your whole heart to the Lord, forsake the wretched world, and your soul will find rest.

Learn to turn your back on mere appearances; give yourself to the development of the inner life. Then you will see the kingdom of God coming to you.

Welcome the kingdom of God as peace and joy in the Holy Spirit.

—John Wesley's edition of Thomas à Kempis'
The Christian's Pattern, 1746

DON'T TALK TOO MUCH

Leave the tumult of the world as much as you can, because we quickly get defiled and taken in by vanity.

I could wish I had often held my tongue and not sat about talking.

Why do we like conversation so much when, after it's all over, we go off by ourselves and suffer a hurt conscience?

We love talking about what we like most and what we desire; we enjoy talking about what troubles us, too. But often such talk proves superficial and serves no good purpose, and we discover that the comfort we get goes only skin-deep.

Therefore, measure your words by prayer lest you spend your time idly.

When you really ought to speak, talk about what builds up. Devout conversation on spiritual subjects furthers our spiritual growth a great deal, especially if you talk with like-minded people bonded to God.

—John Wesley's edition of Thomas à Kempis'
The Christian's Pattern, 1746

HOW TO READ THE BIBLE

Seek truth, not eloquence, when reading Holy Scripture. Read all Scripture in the spirit in which it was written.

Let the love of pure truth draw you to read.

Don't worry too much about *who* wrote what, but underscore *what* you read.

People pass away, but the truth of the Lord remains forever.

God talks to us in many ways, so that people of all conditionings can get his message.

Our own curiosity often hinders us in reading Scripture so that we spend time talking about mere trivialities.

If you really want to profit, read humbly, simply and faithfully.

Inquire willingly, hearing with silence the words of holy men. Don't turn a deaf ear to the parables of the older writers, for they did not write without reason.

—John Wesley's edition of Thomas à Kempis'
The Christian's Pattern, 1746

HOW TO GET PEACE

We could enjoy a great deal of peace if we would not busy ourselves with the words and behavior of others, others with whom we have no concern. How can you live long in peace when you meddle with the cares of other people, and give little attention to your own needs?

Single-hearted people enjoy much peace.

We tend to give too much attention to our own emotional well-being, and to what merely comes and goes. We tend also to put out the flame of fervent desire to grow better, so we stay cold and indifferent.

When we die to ourselves and disengage from low desires, then we relish divine matters. But our tendency is to turn to human comforts when adversity comes.

Endeavor, like people of courage, to stand in the battle, then feel the assistance of God in heaven. He furnishes us with challenges so we will learn to conquer.

If your religion consists of outward observances, your devotion will quickly come to an end. But lay the axe to the root of your passions and discover rest for your soul!

—John Wesley's edition of Thomas à Kempis'
The Christian's Pattern, 1746

THE USES OF ADVERSITY

We need troubles and crosses. They often make us look inwardly in order to see that security does not come from worldly sources.

We ought to smart under contradiction sometimes; we need to know once in awhile that some think poorly of us, even when we intend well. Then we will more diligently seek God for his witness in our hearts. That's why we must settle ourselves so completely in God that when people turn against us, we know our real Source of comfort.

—John Wesley's edition of Thomas à Kempis'
The Christian's Pattern, 1746

HELP IN TEMPTATIONS

When evil thoughts tempt you, then you understand a whole lot better your need of God.

So long as you live in this world, you will have temptations. That's why Job says that in this life we fight a war.

Take care; put your antennae out, pray so you will not get caught in the devil's deceptive clutches. He does not sleep and always goes about seeking someone to devour.

Temptations help us, aggravating though they appear, for in them we progress in humility, purification and instruction.

All saints passed through temptations and tribulations. Those who could not stand up to them fell away and became reprobates.

You cannot find a place so secret that you will have no temptations.

—John Wesley's edition of Thomas à Kempis'
The Christian's Pattern, 1746

HOW TEMPTATIONS BEGIN

Temptations begin with an inconsistent mind and little confidence in God. A ship without its rudder tosses with the waves; a person negligent in keeping his convictions intact experiences temptations of many kinds. But just as fire tempers iron, so temptation makes a strong person.

(We do not always know our gifts and what we can do, but temptations show us our capabilities.)

We must open our eyes, especially at the beginning of a temptation when we can conquer it more readily. But let the Tempter enter your heart's door, and you cannot resist him as you could have at the gate and at the first knock. That's why someone said, "Hold your ground at the outset because remedy afterwards comes too late."

First comes a simple evil thought, then strong imagination, afterward delight, lastly consent. Little by little the malicious enemy gets entrance because it was not resisted at the start.

The longer you play with a temptation, the weaker you become, and the stronger the enemy grows against you.

Some suffer the greatest temptation just after conversion, others later. Some have troubles all through their lives. Some never have very much temptation. In any case, pray fervently to God who gives, with the temptation, a way of escape.

—John Wesley's edition of Thomas à Kempis'
The Christian's Pattern, 1746

Week Seventeen

We should intend God's glory
in every action . . . as St. Paul says,
"Whether you eat or drink, do
all to the glory of God."

John Wesley

WHO PRACTICES THE PRESENCE OF GOD?

The one who walks in the presence of God and talks to him about all needs, asks counsel in every doubting, lets him know all wants, weeps for sins, asks support in weakness, respects him as Judge, reverences him as Lord, obeys him as a Father, and loves him as a Friend—that one practices the presence of God.

—John Wesley's edition of Jeremy Taylor's
The Rules and Exercises of Holy Living, 1750

HOW TO KEEP YOUR FREEDOM

Do not allow yourself to come under the power of anything at all, even good things. "All things are lawful for me, but I will not be brought under the power of any," said St. Paul. To allow yourself impatient desire of anything, so that you cannot abstain from it, is to lose your liberty and to become a servant of food, drink, smoking, or whatever. I wish people would consider this because some don't really suspect themselves guilty of intemperance.

—John Wesley's edition of Jeremy Taylor's
The Rules and Exercises of Holy Living, 1750

KEEP YOURSELF
SEXUALLY PURE

Chastity is the grace that forbids and resists fornication, unnatural sexual behavior, adultery, incest. Chastity means keeping the body and soul pure, in the state God made us, whether of the single or married life.

St. Paul describes the duty of chastity like this: "For this is the will of God, even your sanctification, that you should abstain from fornication; that every one of you should know how to possess yourself in cleanness and honor, not in lust. . . ."

Flee from places and situations that tempt you, like loose company.

If an unclean spirit assaults you, don't trust yourself alone, but run to good people whose reverence and modesty may suppress the spirit, or whose company many divert your thoughts. Their very conversation witnesses against vice, and in that atmosphere your temptation may evaporate in open air, since light and witness have a way of sending evil thoughts away.

—John Wesley's edition of Jeremy Taylor's
The Rules and Exercises of Holy Living, 1750

BE CONTENT

Contentedness in all situations is a duty of religion; it is the great reasonableness of complying with divine Providence, which governs all the world and orders the administration of his great family.

You would come across as a strange fool if you worried that dogs and sheep have no shoes. God supplies animals with foot protection naturally, but you must find artificial means to care for your feet. God gives you the powers of reason to learn to make your own shoes or to buy them. His method of providence differs for you and the animals.

All these gifts come from him, and if we complain, we may next have a troubled mind because God did not make us angels or stars.

If what we are or have or do does not content us, we may make ourselves anxious about everything else in the world.

—John Wesley's edition of Jeremy Taylor's
The Rules and Exercises of Holy Living, 1750

EVERYTHING HAS A
DOUBLE HANDLE

When something happens to displease you, turn it into spiritual advantage. Use it. Nothing exists that does not have a double handle.

For example, when an enemy reproaches you, look on him as a source of impartial critique, for he will tell you more truly than your closest friend about your faults. In that way, what you hear becomes precious, even though you feel like your head will break.

While you forgive your enemy's anger, you make use of his plain speech. If you learn nothing else than to walk and step carefully, how much better than to hear flattery, which turns into pride and carelessness.

—John Wesley's edition of Jeremy Taylor's
The Rules and Exercises of Holy Living, 1750

PREPARE YOUR MIND
FOR CHANGES

Prepare your mind against changes. Always expect them. Then you won't go into shock when they come.

You will never have a bigger enemy of a contented spirit than unreadiness and lack of thought about change. If ready, your change of fortune will not change your spirit. The secret: always stand ready for sorrows.

"O death, how bitter you are to one at rest in his possessions!" The rich man who promised himself ease and a full life for many years, what a sad day when those dreams came to a halt! The first night in eternity, all this hit him by surprise.

But the apostles, who every day knocked at the gate of death and looked on it continually, went to their martyrdom in peace and evenness.

—John Wesley's edition of Jeremy Taylor's
The Rules and Exercises of Holy Living, 1750

A SECRET OF CONTENTMENT

If you want to insure a contented spirit, you must measure your desires by your fortune, not your fortune by your desires. That is, be governed by your needs, not your fancy.

Do you think the animal that has two or three mountains to graze on stands in a better position than a little bee feeding on dew and living on what falls every morning from the storehouses of heaven, clouds, and Providence?

Can one quench his thirst better from a fountain paved with marble than from a spring swelling up from the green turf?

Pride and artificial gluttonies only adulterate nature, making our diet healthless, our appetites impatient and unsatisfiable. But what we sometimes misdefine as poverty may well be the best instrument of contentment.

—John Wesley's edition of Jeremy Taylor's
The Rules and Exercises of Holy Living, 1750

Week Eighteen

❧

God intends troubles should be
the nursery of virtue, the exercise
of wisdom, the trial of patience,
the venturing for a crown and
the gate of glory.

John Wesley

THE BENEFITS OF AFFLICTION

Give thought to affliction as a school of virtue. It reduces our spirits to soberness, and makes our considerations more modest. It corrects levity and interrupts our confidence in sinning.

"It is good for me," said David, "that I have been afflicted, for thereby I have learned your law;" and "I know, O Lord, that you, in faithfulness, caused me to be troubled."

God, who in mercy and wisdom governs the world, would never have allowed so many sadnesses, especially to the wisest and most virtuous people, except that God intends troubles should be the nursery of virtue, the exercise of wisdom, the trial of patience, the venturing for a crown, and the gate of glory.

—John Wesley's edition of Jeremy Taylor's
The Rules and Exercises of Holy Living, 1750

THE DUTIES OF PARENTS
TO CHILDREN

1. **F**athers, do not provoke your children to anger."
Treat them empathetically and gently, adjusting to
children as they are, according to their age level,
meeting their needs.

2. "Bring them up in the nurture and admonition of the
Lord." Give them the principles of genuine religion,
showing love and truth until they become habits; in
that way, before they know good from evil, their
choices may be less dangerous and without so much
difficulty.

3. Show, by example, true religion in the home. Your
behavior is the key. Active love endears you to one
another, and that love takes expressions like pleasant
conversation, affability, frequent admonition. That all
shows your tenderness, care and watchfulness. Then
children look on you as their friends and defence,
their treasure and guide.

4. Parents must provide for their own, enabling the
children to learn a good trade, or the arts, whatever,
so they can defend themselves against the world, not
exposing themselves to temptation, begging, or
unworthy employment.

5. Remember that you can do no greater injury to your
children than to bind them to one another with cords
of disagreement, so they grow to adulthood condi-
tioned by warped love.

—John Wesley's edition of Jeremy Taylor's
The Rules and Exercises of Holy Living, 1750

HOW TO INCREASE FAITH

1. A humble, willing, docile mind; that is, a real desire to let God instruct you—that's the beginning—because persuasion enters like a sunbeam, gently and without violence. Open the window and draw the curtain, and the Sun of Righteousness will enlighten your darkness.

2. Remove all desire to love that which contradicts faith. A sexually immoral person cannot easily believe that without purity no one sees God. One who loves riches too much can hardly accept the truth that surrender of wealth and renunciation of the world, opens one's mind to God. Giving money to God's work and the willingness to die for him—that's folly to the one who attaches him or herself to ease and pleasure instead of the Cross. So the bottom line: if one believes anything contrary to faith, discipleship cannot come very easily.

3. Prayer, instrumental to everything, carries a special promise: "He who lacks wisdom only needs to ask for it" (Jas. 1:5), and "If you give good things to your children, how much more will your heavenly Father give his Spirit to those who ask him?" (Lk. 11:13)

4. In temptation, don't argue; throw yourself on God. Do that with a spiritual mentor, a wise and untempted guide. Be sure of this: all changes of belief that offer themselves in your time of greatest weakness, and that contradict your best thinking—well, reject them!

—John Wesley's edition of Jeremy Taylor's
The Rules and Exercises of Holy Living, 1750

HOW TO INCREASE HOPE

1. Rely on God with confident expectation that his promises will come true. "Every degree of hope is a degree of confidence."

2. Understand that every danger, crisis, or accident does not document a defect on God's part, but is either a mercy from God or a fault of our own. Then you will certainly trust God because you see him as your confidence. "The hope of a Christian is prudent and religious."

3. Rejoice in the midst of a misfortune or sadness, knowing that this may work for good, and will if your soul lives in tune with God. To look through the clouds and see a beam of light from God—that's a direct act of hope. Scripture calls this "rejoicing in tribulation" when "the God of hope fills us with joy in believing." Every degree of hope brings a degree of joy.

4. Desire, pray, and long for the great object of our hope, the mighty prize of our high calling. Desire other things in life insofar as they bring glory to God and our souls to their intended end. We have a saying that hope and fasting are the two wings of prayer. Fasting is like the wing of a bird, but hope like the wing of an angel soaring up to heaven, bearing our prayers to the throne of grace.

—John Wesley's edition of Jeremy Taylor's
The Rules and Exercises of Holy Living, 1750

LOVE

Love is the greatest thing that God can give us, for he himself is love. Love is the greatest thing we can give to God, for it also includes giving ourselves and all that is ours.

Love does the work of all other graces, without any instrument but its own immediate virtue. As the love of sin makes one sin against all one's own reason and all arguments of wisdom and advice of friends, so love of God makes one chaste, and temperate, and reaches toward glory through the very heart of grace, without any other arms but those of love.

Grace loves God for himself, and our neighbors for God. Thinking about God's goodness and bounty comes from love. But when we once enter into the world of love and have tasted the goodness of God, we pass from passion to reason, from thanking to adoring, from sense to spirit, from ourselves to union with God.

Love is the image and little hint of heaven; it is happiness in picture, or rather the infancy and beginnings of glory.

—John Wesley's edition of Jeremy Taylor's
The Rules and Exercises of Holy Living, 1750

HOW CHRISTIANS FACE DEATH

When a good person dies, one who lived innocently or made joy in heaven by repentance (in whose defence the angels drive away the devils on the death bed), who lived life in Christ consistently, even when tempted— well, at the time of death, joys break through clouds of sickness, the conscience stands upright, and the spirit confesses the glories of God.

Just then the sorrows of sickness, the flames of fever, the weakness from disease serve to untie the soul from its chain and free it first to freedom, then to glory.

Only for a little while did the face of the sky appear black, but the clouds quickly tore themselves away, the violence of thunder split into bits and pieces, so the sun could come out and shine without a tear.

—John Wesley's edition of Jeremy Taylor's
The Rules and Exercises of Holy Living, 1750

WHAT HAPPENS IN DEATH

What an infinite refreshment to remember all the comforts of prayer, the frequent victories over temptation, the killing of lusts, the sacrifices for God, the giving over of the will to him for his service! All trouble now gone, God makes way for the inheritance Jesus gives, now no longer distant, but soon to be reality.

When death comes, prison doors open and release the dying to the presence of God's angel. The soul goes full of hope and instantly passes into the company of spirits, where singing angels meet that soul, even though the devils flock with malicious and vile purposes, desiring to lead it away with them into their houses of sorrow. The soul goes right forward, rejoicing, triumphant, passing the devils, securely carried to the Lord where it feasts, makes music, rejoices and worships for ever and ever.

—John Wesley's edition of Jeremy Taylor's
The Rules and Exercises of Holy Living, 1750

Week Nineteen

Do you want to know the
greatest saint in the world?
You will not find him or her
the one who prays most, nor fasts
most, nor gives most, nor exercises
temperance, chastity or justice
most. You will find the greatest
saint the one always
thankful to God.

John Wesley

SINGING PSALMS

Begin your prayers with a psalm. I do not mean you should read over a psalm, but that you chant or sing one.

You will easily understand the difference between singing and reading a psalm if you consider the difference between reading or singing a common song you like. While you read it, you will only like it, but as soon as you sing it, you feel the same spirit within you that the words themselves carry.

You may say you cannot sing. A good objection if you sing to entertain others, but not a good objection for singing God's praises in private.

Live in such a way that your heart truly rejoices in God, that your being itself flows with praises. Then you will find that both your voice and ear make tunes for a psalm.

—John Wesley's edition of William Law's
A Serious Call to a Devout and Holy Life, 1744

THE GREATEST SAINT

Do you want to know the greatest saint in the world? You will not find him or her the one who prays most, nor fasts most, nor gives most; nor exercises temperance, chastity or justice most. You will find the greatest saint the one always thankful to God, who wills whatever God wills, who receives everything as the gift of God's goodness, with a heart always ready to praise him.

The purpose of all our devotions, fastings, repentance, meditations, quiet times, and sacraments—we do all these to become more conformable to God's will and act more thankfully. Herein lies the perfection of all virtues, and all virtues that do not relate to it or proceed from it prove so many false ornaments of a soul not really converted to God.

—John Wesley's edition of William Law's
A Serious Call to a Devout and Holy Life, 1744

THE SHORTEST, SUREST WAY TO HAPPINESS

The shortest, surest way to happiness is to thank and praise God for every thing that happens to you. For whatever seeming calamity takes place, if you thank and praise God for it, you turn it into a blessing.

Do you want to work miracles? You could do no more for yourself than by this thankful spirit because it heals with a word and turns all it touches into happiness.

Thankfulness is the purpose of all true religion. Settle your mind, that this posture reflects your aim in all devotions. Once fixed, you have something plain and visible to walk by, something to measure your spirituality by. Insofar as you renounce your own self-will, seeking no other happiness but thankful reception of all that happens to you, you have advanced in spirituality.

This attitude does not depend on time, place or a great occasion, but always lies in your power to exercise daily.

—John Wesley's edition of William Law's
A Serious Call to a Devout and Holy Life, 1744

FOOLISH REASON

Our misery lies in this: we borrow the powers of our nature to torment and vex ourselves and our fellow creatures.

God entrusts us with reason, but we use it to disorder and corrupt ourselves. We reason ourselves into all kinds of folly and misery, and make our lives the sport of foolish and extravagant emotions, seeking after imaginary happiness of all kinds, creating a thousand wants, amusing our hearts with false hopes and fears, turning the world into worse than irrational animals, envying, vexing, tormenting one another with restless passions and unreasonable contentions.

In this way we sully and corrupt our best actions. But turn your eyes toward heaven. God stands prepared to take away our guilt.

—John Wesley's edition of William Law's
A Serious Call to a Devout and Holy Life, 1744

PUT THE WORLD
INTO PERSPECTIVE

To lessen your regard to the opinion of the world, think how soon the world will disregard you and have no more thought or concern about you than about the poorest animal that died in a ditch.

Your friends, if they can, may bury you with some distinction, and set up a monument to let posterity see that your dust lies under such a stone. But when that is done, all is done. Another soon fills your place. The world is just in the same state it was. Blotted from sight, you no longer find a place in the world . . . as if you had never belonged to it.

—John Wesley's edition of William Law's
A Serious Call to a Devout and Holy Life, 1744

HOLY INTERCESSION

Holy intercession raised the early Christians to a state of mutual love. That love created a friendship far above all other ancient friendships.

When that same spirit of intercession invades the world again, holy friendship will come into fashion. Once more, Christians will stand out as the wonder of the world.

Why? Frequent intercession with God, earnestly beseeching him to forgive the sins of all persons, to bless them with his providence, to enlighten them with his Spirit, and bring them to everlasting happiness—that constitutes the divinest exercise the human heart can engage in.

—John Wesley's edition of William Law's
A Serious Call to a Devout and Holy Life, 1744

PERSONAL BENEFITS OF
PRAYING FOR OTHERS

o to your knees daily, in solemn, deliberate devotion. Pray for others with such length, urgency and earnestness as you pray for yourself.

Then you will find that all little, ill-natured emotions die. Your heart will delight in the common happiness of others, even though you used to delight only in your own happiness.

Shape your intercessions to the needs of your friends pleading with God to deliver them from specific evils, to grant them special gifts. In addition to the great love of your neighbors that such intercession creates, you will notice a mighty effect on your own heart.

—John Wesley's edition of William Law's
A Serious Call to a Devout and Holy Life, 1744

Week Twenty

Nothing makes us love our neighbors more than praying for them.

John Wesley

A HOLY MINISTER

Uranius is a holy minister, full of the spirit of the gospel, watching, laboring, and praying for a poor country village. Every soul in it is as dear to him as himself, and he loves them all as he loves himself. Proof? He prays for them all as often as he prays for himself.

He invests his whole life in continual zeal and labor, never quite satisfied with his degree of care. He learned the great value of souls; that explains why he comes to God with his parishioners so often.

He never thinks he can love or do enough for his flock. He believes his hope, joy and crown of rejoicing lies in God gifting and gracing them.

He goes about his parish, visiting each person in it. He visits in the same spirit of piety that he preaches; he visits to encourage their virtues, to assist them with advice to discover their style of life, and to know the status of their souls so he can intercede according to their specific necessities.

—John Wesley's edition of William Law's
A Serious Call to a Devout and Holy Life, 1744

GIFTED PRAY-ERS

The prayers of persons recognized for holiness have an extraordinary power with God. God grants to such people blessings through their prayers that he would not grant to others of less piety.

This explains, in people seeking perfection, why they search for every grace, a holy temper, care in behavior lest their prayers not avail very much with God. This also explains why such pray-ers monitor every temper of their hearts, give alms to all they can, observe, fast, die to self, live according to the strictest rules of temperance, meekness and humility. This, they hope, will make them in some degree like an Abraham or a Job, so that God will hear prayers and answer them.

We should all emulate this example.

—John Wesley's edition of William Law's
A Serious Call to a Devout and Holy Life, 1744

THE POWER AND SECRET
OF HUMILITY

Pride makes persons hateful; humility makes them lovable. Modesty, in a sense, forces esteem. We couldn't possibly despise the most common or greatest person who has humility.

So how do we get it? By seeing ourselves learners. For we must learn something quite contrary to our former self and habits.

Not only do we have much to learn, we have a great deal to unlearn: a whole set of attitudes, fixed and formed, fashioned after the world. Our value system, warped and skewed, must undergo radical change.

> —John Wesley's edition of William Law's
> *A Serious Call to a Devout and Holy Life,* 1744

WHAT HAPPENS WHEN
FATHERS PRAY?

When fathers daily pray specifically for their children, that they may live in true piety, with great humility and the disciplines of temperance, what could be more likely than to make the father himself model those virtues? Naturally he will grow embarrassed at his lack of Christian traits, the very traits he prays for his children.

The bottom line: his prayers for their spirituality become a certain means of lifting his own spirituality.

—John Wesley's edition of William Law's
A Serious Call to a Devout and Holy Life, 1744

HOW TO STOP
NEGATIVE FEELINGS

When you feel the first approaches of resentment, envy, or contempt toward others; when you think of little disagreements and misunderstandings; instead of indulging your mind with little, low reflections, pray specifically for the people who made you think envy, resentment or discontent. This definitely prevents the growth of all uncharitable feelings.

Tailor prayers to the degree of your negativity and you will mend your heart.

For instance, when you sense envy toward any person, because of wealth, power, reputation, learning, advancement, then immediately pray God to bless and prosper that person in everything that stimulated your envy. Repeat your prayer, praying with all earnestness for complete happiness from their blessings, then you will soon find this prayer the best medicine to expel the venom that attacks your soul.

This kind of praying removes all peevishness, softens your heart into the greatest tenderness, and becomes the best arbitrator of any differences between you and the person who threatened you.

—John Wesley's edition of William Law's
A Serious Call to a Devout and Holy Life, 1744

WATCH OUT FOR THE
SUSURRUS EFFECT!

Susurrus is a pious, temperate man, remarkable for his many excellent qualities. He never misses a church service. He almost starves himself so he can give more money to the poor.

But he has one terrible failing. He likes to hear and discover defects in everyone around him. He welcomes tidbits about everybody, so long as you do not talk like an enemy. He never dislikes an evil speaker unless the language gets rough and emotional. Just whisper gently something ever so bad, and Susurrus receives it readily.

When he visits, you generally hear him relating how sorry he feels for the failings of his neighbor. He lets you know how tender his own heart is for the reputation of his neighbor, how hesitant he is to say what he feels forced to say, and how gladly he would conceal the gossip if only he could conceal it.

Susurrus has such a tender, compassionate manner in relating things terribly prejudicial against his neighbor, that he even seems, both to himself and others, to be exercising Christian charity at the very time he indulges his whispering, evil temper.

—John Wesley's edition of William Law's
A Serious Call to a Devout and Holy Life, 1744

HOW GOD CURED SUSURRUS

Susurrus once whispered to a friend, in great secrecy, something too bad to speak in public. He ended by saying how glad he felt that not many had heard about it, and that he had some hopes of its falsity, though he suspected it true.

Susurrus' friend replied like this: "Susurrus, you say you're glad few know about this and hope it's not true. Therefore, go home to a private place and pray for this man with as much earnestness as you would pray for yourself in such a situation. Plead with God to favor the man, to save him from false accusers, and to bring shame on all those who tell bad things about him. After all, these uncharitable whisperers, telling secret stories, wound him as if stabbed in the dark."

This really got through to Susurrus because he felt the sting of rebuke. His conscience troubled him just as much as if the books had opened on him at the Day of Judgment. Susurrus realized he could not accept or reject the criticism without self-condemnation.

From that time to this, he has prayed faithfully for those he might have gossiped about. He has undergone complete change. He simply cannot privately whisper anything to prejudice someone against another any more than he could pray that God would hurt someone.

—John Wesley's edition of William Law's
A Serious Call to a Devout and Holy Life, 1744

Week Twenty-One

O might we all, like him, believe,
And keep the faith and win
the Prize!

Charles Wesley

ON THE DEATH OF THE REVEREND MR. JAMES HERVEY, DECEMBER 25, 1758*

He's gone! the spotless soul is gone
   Triumphant to his place above;
The prison walls are broken down,
   The angels speed his swift remove,
And shouting on their wings he flies,
And Hervey rests in paradise.

Saved by the merit of his Lord,
   Salvation, praise to Christ he gives,
Yet still his merciful reward
   According to his works receives;
And with the seed he sow'd below,
His joy eternally shall *grow.*

—Charles Wesley's poem on the death of
James Hervey, December 25, 1758

* In the 18th century death became the motif of English culture. Stories, poems, press articles—every medium— picked up the theme. Evangelical Christians concerned themselves with preparation for death and the celebration of godly people who died in the Lord. John Wesley declared that Methodists die well.

James Hervey was a leading evangelical preacher.

CHARLES WESLEY'S PRAYER ON THE DEATH OF JAMES HERVEY

Through Jesu's name, and strength, and word,
    The well-fought fight our brother won;
Arm'd with the Savior's blood and sword,
    He cast the dire accuser down,
Compell'd the aliens to submit,
And trampled flesh beneath his feet.

O may we all, like him, believe,
    And keep the faith, and win the prize!
Father, prepare, and then receive
    Our hallow'd spirits to the skies,
To chant, with all our friends above,
Your glorious everlasting love.

—Charles Wesley

THANKSGIVING FOR AN ESCAPE FROM BEING CRUSHED TO DEATH

November 8, 1782

Thee, Father, I praise,
Almighty in grace,
Your power be acknowledged, your mercy adored!
In dangers and snares
Thou number'st my hairs,
Your wings are outspread,
My soul to defend, and to cover my head.

When destruction was nigh,
I was under Thine eye;
When the ruin came down,
Unconscious of harm, and unhurt, I went on:
Without your decree
No evil could be,
And, restrain'd by your will,
Death himself had no power, or commission, to kill.

Reserved by the love
Of my Savior above,
Your servant I am,
Your kingdom to spread, and to hallow your name:
Thee in Jesus to know,
And publish below
Your unspeakable grace,
Which abolishes death, and redeems our whole race.

For this at your feet
Expecting I sit,
Till your counsel Thou show,
And discover the work Thou wouldst have me to do:
Whatsoever it be,
Let me do it to Thee,
And your blessing receive,
And an heir of your kingdom eternally live.

—Charles Wesley

Note: Charles Wesley (1707-1788) experienced a great deal of mob violence; curious readers may want to consult Arnold A. Dallimore, *A Heart Set Free: The Life of Charles Wesley* (Westchester, Ill.: Crossway Books, 1988). John Simon, in his *The Revival of Religion in the Eighteenth Century,* observes, "With a superb courage . . . the Methodist preachers went again and again, to the places from which they had been driven by violence, until their persistence wore down the antagonism of their assailants. Then, out of the once furious crowd, men and women were gathered whose hearts the Lord had touched."

A PRAYER FOR COURAGE

Let none forsake the fold, and fly,
Let none through fear their Lord deny,
    But stand the fiery hour;
The greatness of your mercy prove,
The truth of your redeeming love,
    And all-sufficient power.

Let none unwarily give place
To Satan, with his angel face,
    And yield their souls to sell;
To sell their conscience and their God,
Or, weary, leave the narrow road,
    And go for ease—to hell.

Now, Savior, now their fears remove;
The sense of your forgiving love
    Abundantly impart
To all whose sacred load we feel;
The prayer of faith this moment seal
    On every panting heart.

—Charles Wesley, *Selections from the Poetry Illustrative of his
Journal and Correspondence,* 1870

CELEBRATION OF A
LIFE WELL LIVED

O that the child of heavenly light
Might drop her mantle in her flight,
   Her lamb-like spirit leave!
On us let all her graces rest,
To make meek every troubled breast,
   And teach us how to grieve.

Happy could we the secret find,
Like her in all events resign'd,
   To gain by every loss;
Our sharpest agonies to improve,
Esteem our Master's lot, and love,
   And glory in his cross.

Made ready here, by patient love,
For sweetest fellowship above
   With our translated friend,
Give us through life her spirit to breathe,
Indulge us then to die her death,
   And bless us with her end.

—Charles Wesley reflecting "On the death of
Mrs. L_____ ," July 6, 1756

A "FEAST" TO REFRESH
THE BODY

Monday morning, February 8th, took my horse toward Tyril's-pass. We overtook a lad whistling one of our tunes. He joined us in several hymns we knew by heart.

Near seven, we arrived, half choked with fog, at Mr. Force's. The town immediately crowded around us. I spoke on "A certain man had two sons." Never have I spoken to more hungry souls. They devoured every word. Some expressed their happiness by whistling for joy! Few such feasts have I had since I left England. It refreshed my body more than meat or drink.

—Charles Wesley's *Journal*, February 8, 1748

JOY AND TEMPTATION

esterday I saw Mrs. Bird. At her baptism she was quite overpowered, and struck speechless. Now she tells me, in going home that night, such joy sprang up in her heart as she never felt before, a joy full of heaven. It lasted all night.

Since then, she has suffered fright at the withdrawal, at least the abatement, of her happiness. I told her she must expect temptation as well as comfort, that immediately following our Lord's baptism came temptation.

—Charles Wesley, letter to his wife, July 1, 1756

Week Twenty-Two

It is impossible to be a true
Christian and an enemy
at the same time.

John Wesley

CHRISTIAN HOLINESS

The Bible tells us that God is love, and those who love, live in God, but those who do not live in love, do not live in God. It is impossible to be a true Christian and an enemy at the same time. Humankind has only one enemy, the devil and those who follow him.

To love instead of hate comes easily to those born of God, but to those not born of God, loving enemies is perhaps the biggest difficulty.

Here we see Christian holiness and the godlike spirit it implies. God changes us to desire only what he desires. When we rejoice and delight only in God, we love our fellow creatures.

—John Wesley's edition of William Law's
Christian Perfection, 1754

HOW TO LEARN AS A CHILD

Our Savior said to let the little children come to him, for of such is the kingdom of God. If we do not deceive ourselves, we become like infants, with everything to learn. We can be taught what to choose and what to avoid. We should assume no wisdom, and believe God stands ready to teach us the only way to find happiness. God calls us to accept wisdom with the simplicity of children who have nothing of their own to compete with it. With child-like openness, then, we give ourselves to Christ to govern us.

The craft, selfish cunning, pride and vanity of the world have no admittance into the holy society of Christ. The wisdom of this world, the intrigues of life, the designs of greatness and ambition lead to another kingdom. Those who follow Christ must be emptied of this vain furniture; they put on the ornament of infant simplicity.

—John Wesley's edition of William Law's
Christian Perfection, 1754

MERE OUTWARD RELIGION

Those content with outward religion, those whose Christianity lies only in outward decency, miss the genuine product. These people find themselves content with anything short of newness of heart, lacking the Holy Spirit that the gospel describes.

Those who take this stance should observe that charity, chastity, sobriety and justice can be practiced without Christianity. A pagan may prove charitable and temperate, but to make these qualities Christian they must come from a heart truly turned to God, a heart truly crucified with Christ, born again of his Spirit, who overcomes the world.

—John Wesley's edition of William Law's
Christian Perfection, 1754

IN WHAT DOES
CHRISTIANITY CONSIST?

man who was a drunkard for many years thinks he made a sufficient change by becoming temperate. Another imagines he enjoys good spiritual status because he does not neglect public worship as he used to. A lady supposes she stands at a higher level religiously because she now selects her entertainment better.

But such people should consider that Christianity does not consist in having fewer vices than others nor in living by some particular virtue nor yet in the revision of behavior. It does consist in a thorough change of heart, the change that makes the love of God the spring, measure and rule of our attitudes and actions.

—John Wesley's edition of William Law's
Christian Perfection, 1754

REAL RELIGION

Real religion lifts us into a new world, puts fresh goals into our lives, takes possession of our hearts, alters the whole tune of our minds, changes the entire stream of our affections, gives us joys and griefs, hopes and fears. Everything becomes new in true religion.

God saturates our hearts with his love; he does that by the Holy Spirit in us. This Spirit bears witness with our spirits that we are the children of God, which makes us Christians not in name only, but in truth. So we do in fact believe in the holy Jesus, and when he comes again, we will rejoice in that Day of Christ because we have not run life's race in vain.

—John Wesley's edition of William Law's
Christian Perfection, 1754

TWO GREAT TRUTHS

Two great truths undergird the gospel: the deplorable corruption of human nature, and new birth in Christ Jesus. One includes all the misery of the human family, the other, all the happiness of humanity.

The frame of Christianity builds on these two truths, forbidding whatever fastens us to the disorders of sin, and commanding only those duties that lead us into the liberty of the sons of God. This explains how Christians behave and why they cherish the inspirations of the Inner Voice. Christians open their minds to the divine light and move resolutely toward the righteous life of the new birth.

—John Wesley's edition of William Law's
Christian Perfection, 1754

CHRISTIAN BEHAVIOR

All true Christians continually work at behaving themselves righteously. Christians stand in awe of God, and keep an eagle eye out for evil. They pray with a kind of desperation, knowing that yielding to temptation can carry them to the brink of eternal death or death itself.

Christians believe, hope, work and aspire to the best moral standard. They sense their call to fight the good fight of faith, to lay hold on eternal life.

—John Wesley's edition of William Law's
Christian Perfection, 1754

Week Twenty-Three

I worked very hard at teaching family religion, the heart's desire of Methodists. In time many... adopted Joshua's resolution, "As for me and my house, we will serve the Lord."

John Wesley

WEALTH FOR YOUR CHILDREN?

Do not allow anyone to deceive you with vain words; riches and happiness seldom live together. Therefore, if you want wisdom, you will not seek wealth for your children by marriage. Double check your vision: keep an eye single to the glory of God, and, therefore, the real happiness of your children both in this life and the next.

—John Wesley's sermon, "On Family Religion," 1783

ALL POLYGAMY FORBIDDEN

Marriage is holy and honorable. Jesus said that anyone who puts away his wife except for fornication causes her to commit adultery. If, under those circumstances, she marries again, her new mate commits adultery.

Jesus forbids all polygamy when he declares that if any woman marries while her husband still lives, she commits adultery. By the same token, any man who marries while his wife lives, commits adultery. A man will not commit adultery when he remarries, even though his wife still lives, if her adultery caused the divorce.

—John Wesley's sermon, "Upon Our Lord's Sermon on the Mount, III," 1748

WHO MUST GET YOUR ATTENTION?

The person in your house who claims your first and nearest attention is, undoubtedly, your wife. The Bible says you must love her as Christ loves his church; he laid down his life for the church to purify it. A husband must pursue the same goal, helping his wife at every turn to live freed from sin, and liberated to walk unblamably in love.

Next to your wife, your children must get love and attention. God has, for a time, entrusted them to your care, to train them up in all holiness and equip them for the enjoyment of God in eternity. What a glorious and important trust! Especially since one soul counts for more value than all the world. You must, therefore, watch over every child with utmost care; some day God the Father will call on you to give account of each one. You will want to give your accounting with joy, not grief.

—John Wesley's sermon, "On Family Religion," 1783

ONLY GOD CAN HELP YOU
WITH YOUR FAMILY

Undoubtedly, if you determine consistently to walk the path of righteousness with your family, to endeavor by every possible means to serve the Lord, to encourage every member of your family to worship God not only in form but in spirit and in truth . . . if you aim at all that, you will need to use all the grace and courage, and all the wisdom God has given you. For you will find such hindrances in the way, that only the mighty power of God can enable you to break through to success.

—John Wesley's sermon, "On Family Religion," 1783

THE EDUCATION OF CHILDREN

few have dared to leave the common road and educate their children in a Christian manner. Some tutors at the university have educated the children under their care and after a style worthy of the early Christians.

—John Wesley's letter, "To the Society *Pro Fide et Christianismo,*" December 23, 1775

CLUES TO A SOUND MARRIAGE

ave you both the consent of your parents? Without this, there is seldom a blessing.

Secondly, you must ask if your intended husband is able to take care of you; I mean in the way you have lived up to now. Otherwise, remember!, when poverty comes in at the door, love flies out at the window.

—John Wesley, *Letters,* to Jane Hilton, October 8, 1768

STRONG FAMILY CONVICTIONS

worked very hard at teaching family religion, the heart's desire of Methodists. In time many, after suffering shame before God about family attitudes, adopted Joshua's resolution, "As for me and my house, we will serve the Lord."

—John Wesley's *Journal*, Sunday, November 16, 1766

Week Twenty-Four

Here [Acts 5] we have a native specimen of a New Testament church: A company of men and women called by the gospel, grafted into Christ by baptism, animated by love, united by all kinds of fellowship, and disciplined by the death of Ananias and Sapphira.

John Wesley

WHO IDENTIFIES WITH
THE CHURCH?

The Apostle Paul tells the Ephesians that church people assemble themselves for the worship of God the Father and his Son, Jesus Christ. St. Paul sees the church as one body everywhere.

One Spirit brings life to all Christians. The Holy Spirit is the Fountain of all spiritual life. The Bible clearly states that if one does not have the Spirit of Christ, he or she cannot belong to him. God's "one Spirit" also gives spiritual gifts to the members of his church.

—John Wesley's sermon, "Of the Church," 1785

ONE HOPE

All who receive the "one Spirit," receive "one hope," the hope of eternal life. They know that to die does not mean to be lost. Their prospect extends beyond the grave. They can cheerfully say, "Blessed be the God and Father of our Lord Jesus Christ who, according to his abundant mercy, has brought us a lively hope by the resurrection of Jesus Christ from the dead, to an inheritance incorruptible and undefiled which will not fade away."

—John Wesley's sermon, "Of the Church," 1785

ONE LORD

Those who accept the one Spirit have one Lord, one Lord who now has dominion over them. He has set up his kingdom in their hearts and reigns over all those who possess the "one hope." To obey him, to follow the way of his commands, is their glory and joy. And while they do this with a willing mind, they "sit in heavenly places with Christ Jesus."

—John Wesley's sermon, "Of the Church," 1785

ONE FAITH

Our one faith, the free gift of God, is the ground of our hope. This faith is not merely the bare faith of the heathen. We believe in the existence of God, gracious, just and the rewarder of those who diligently seek him. Neither is it only the bare faith of the devil who believes both the Old and New Testaments. Rather, it is the faith of St. Thomas who said with holy boldness, "My Lord and my God!" This faith enables every true Christian believer to testify with St. Paul, "The life which I now live, I live by faith in the Son of God, who loved me, and gave himself for me."

—John Wesley's sermon, "Of the Church," 1783

ONE BAPTISM

The church accepts one baptism, the outward sign our one Lord appointed to express the inward and spiritual grace he continually gives his church. Through baptism, God gives faith and hope to those who diligently seek him. Some interpret this in a figurative sense, as if it referred to the baptism of the Holy Spirit, which the apostles received on the day of Pentecost. But Scripture interpretation leads us to stay with the plain, literal sense, unless it implies an absurdity.

—John Wesley's sermon, "Of the Church," 1783

ONE GOD, THE FATHER OF ALL

All who feel adopted sense that they relate to one God, the Father. The Spirit of adoption cries in adopted hearts, "Abba, Father." That cry witnesses continually with their spirits that they are the children of God, the God "who is above all," the Most High, the Creator, the Sustainer, the Governor of the whole universe, pervading all space and filling heaven and earth. In a special way, he lives in his church members, the people of one body who live by one Spirit,

> Making your souls his loved abode,
> The temples of indwelling God.

—John Wesley's sermon, "Of the Church," 1783

HOW, THEN, DO WE DEFINE THE CHURCH?

Here, then, we have a clear answer to the question, "What is the church?" The universal church is all the persons in the universe God has called out of the world, those parts of the "one body," united by the "one Spirit," having "one faith," "one hope," "one baptism," one God the Father of all, who is above all, and through all, and in them all.

—John Wesley's sermon, "Of the Church," 1783

Week Twenty-Five

Toward the end of 1739,
eight or ten persons came to me in
London, appearing deeply
convinced of sin and earnestly
struggling for a remedy.

John Wesley

GROUPS

Toward the end of 1739, eight or ten persons came to me in London, appearing deeply convinced of sin and earnestly struggling for a remedy. They desired (as did two or three more the next day) that I spend some time with them in prayer, and advise them how to flee from the wrath to come, which they saw continually hanging over their heads.

So that we could have more time for this very important work, I appointed a day when they could all come together. They came on that day every week after our first meeting. We met Thursday evenings.

To those who came—the number increased daily—I gave counsel from time to time, counsel I thought most needed. We always concluded our meetings with prayer shaped to persons' needs.

—John Wesley, "The Nature, Design, and General Rules of the United Societies," 1743

THE PURPOSE OF GROUPS

The groups or societies started first in London, then spread to other places. These companies of people

> Take on the pattern of godliness,
> Seek the power of God,
> Unite to pray,
> Receive words of encouragement,
> Watch over one another in love,
> Help each other to work out their salvation.

To make sure each person does in fact work out his or her own salvation, each larger group or society divides into smaller groups, called classes. Where people live geographically determines the location of their smaller group.

—John Wesley, "The Nature, Design, and General Rules of the United Societies," 1743

SMALLER GROUPS

We have about twelve people in these smaller groups or classes. When we make one a leader, he or she has two tasks: (1) To see each person in his class at least once a week, in order to inquire how their souls prosper. He advises, reproves, comforts, counsels—any of that, as needed. He also takes up a collection, insofar as people can give, to help the poor.

(2) The leader meets the minister and the stewards of the larger group, the society, once a week. He tells the minister of any who suffer illness, of any whose walk deviates from the Christian way and who will not take direction. He also gives the stewards the money collected for the poor, and shows an account of what each person gave.

—John Wesley, "The Nature, Design, and General Rules of the United Societies," 1743

GOOD WORKS

Zealously keep doing good works, especially

1. Give money and possessions as much as you can.

2. Reprove all sin and do it in love, meekness and wisdom.

3. Be a pattern of diligence and frugality, of self-denial and of taking up the cross daily.

—John Wesley, "Directions Given to
the Band Societies," 1744

AVOID EVIL

Carefully abstain from evil, especially

1. Refusing to observe the Lord's Day.
2. Drinking liquor of any kind.
3. Dishonesty in buying and selling.
4. Gossip—mentioning faults of another behind his or her back—and stop those who start to gossip.
5. Extravagance in dress.
6. Needless self-indulgence like chewing or smoking tobacco.

—John Wesley, "Directions Given to
the Band Societies," 1744

OBSERVE THE MEANS OF GRACE

Give consistent attention to the means of grace, in particular

1. Church attendance and Holy Communion, and the meetings of your small group.
2. Regular listening to the exposition and reading of the Word of God, daily if possible.
3. Private prayer each day, and family prayers. If you are the head of the family, give leadership to your wife and children in daily devotions.
4. When space comes in the flow of your day, read Scripture and meditate on what you read.
5. Each week fast and exercise abstinence.[*]

—John Wesley, "Directions Given to the Band Societies," 1744

[*] In this passage, Wesley does not indicate from what we should fast (except food), but uses the general word "abstinence." He abstained from a certain amount of buying and selling, from too much talk, from wasting time, etc. Today he would encourage us to abstain from too much food, drink, television, and anything that encourages self-indulgence.

THE MINISTRY

Ministers serve only as instruments in God's hand. They depend entirely on his blessing to give increase to their labors. Without God's blessing, they are nothing.

I pray that all ministers serve in unity with one another. And I pray too that they retain a sense of honor due to God who employs them. They must work faithfully, not for themselves, but for the Great Proprietor of all, until the day comes when he will reward them fully in proportion to their fidelity and diligence.

—John Wesley's *Explanatory Notes Upon the New Testament,* 1755

Week Twenty-Six

I am to show that it is the duty of every Christian to receive the Lord's Supper as often as he or she can.

What is baptism? It is the sacrament which initiates us, which gives us entry into covenant with God.

John Wesley

THE LORD'S SUPPER: CHRIST'S COMMAND

I am to show that it is the duty of every Christian to receive the Lord's Supper as often as he or she can. First, because Christ commands it: "Do this in remembrance of me."

Even as the apostles had to bless, break and give the bread to all who joined them, so Christians must receive those signs of Christ's body and blood.

Remember that Christ commanded his Supper just as he laid down his life for us. In a sense, then, they were his dying words to all his followers.

—John Wesley's sermon, "The Duty of
Constant Communion," 1787

BENEFITS OF HOLY COMMUNION

Christians should take the Lord's Supper as often as possible because of the great benefits. For example, forgiveness of our past sins and the present strengthening and refreshing of our souls. In this world we never free ourselves from temptations. Whatever way of life we walk, whatever our condition, whether sick or well, in trouble or at ease, the enemies of our souls watch for an opportunity to lead us into sin. Too often those enemies win.

Now, when we know we have sinned against God, what surer way do we have of pardon than showing we believe in the power of our Lord's death, beseeching him because of his sufferings to blot out all our sins?

—John Wesley's sermon, "The Duty of Constant Communion," 1787

STRENGTH FROM HOLY COMMUNION

As our bodies grow strong by bread and wine, so our souls, by these tokens of the body and blood of Christ, take on energy. This is food for our souls: strength to perform our duties, grace to move on to perfection.

So if we want power to believe, to love and obey God, we should neglect no opportunity of receiving the Lord's Supper. One who refuses to take Communion either does not understand one's duty, or does not care about the dying command of the Savior. One must see how his Supper provides resource for forgiveness of sins, strength for the soul, and refreshing with hope.

—John Wesley's sermon, "The Duty of
Constant Communion," 1787

PREPARATION FOR
THE LORD'S SUPPER

Whenever time permits, do prepare yourselves for this solemn ordinance by self-examination and prayer.

When we do not have time for special preparation, we should see that we habitually prepare by the way we live; that is absolutely necessary, no matter what the day brings. This ongoing preparation comes with full *purpose* in our hearts to keep all the commandments of God; secondly, by a sincere *desire* to receive all his promises.

—John Wesley's sermon, "The Duty of
Constant Communion," 1787

BAPTISM

In baptism, we, through faith, graft onto Christ. We draw new spiritual life from this new root, through his Spirit who fashions us like himself, especially with regard to his death and resurrection.

—John Wesley's *Explanatory Notes Upon the New Testament,* 1755

THE FIRST BENEFIT OF BAPTISM

What primary benefit do we receive in baptism? Washing away the guilt from original sin. The merits of Christ's death does this.

We all come into the world under the guilt of Adam's sin; all sin deserves eternal misery—the ancient church stood unanimous on that point—but God gives us the free gift of justification. That gift comes to reality in baptism.

—John Wesley, "A Treatise on Baptism," 1756

BAPTISM AND THE CHURCH

By baptism, we secure admittance into the church. That makes us members of Christ, the Head of the church. Even as the Jews came into the church by circumcision, so Christians come in by baptism.

Because we are, then, children of God, we are heirs of the kingdom of heaven. "If children," observes the apostle, "then heirs, heirs of God, and joint-heirs with Christ." We receive title to "a kingdom that cannot be moved."

So baptism saves us now if we live answerable to it, if we repent, believe and obey the gospel. Even as baptism admits us to the church, so later it admits us to eternal glory.

—John Wesley, "A Treatise on Baptism," 1756

Week Twenty-Seven

For what purpose did God
give us life? Why did he
send us into the world?
For one purpose only:
to prepare us for eternity.

John Wesley

WHY DID GOD GIVE US LIFE?

or what purpose did God give us life? Why did he send us into the world? For one purpose only: to prepare us for eternity.

It pleased the all-wise God, at the time he saw best, to show the greatness of his strength by creating the heavens and the earth and all things in them.

"He created human beings in his own image, after his own likeness." And the purpose of creating us? Only this: that we might know, love, enjoy, and serve the Creator throughout eternity.

God did not create you merely to please your senses, to gratify your desires, to make money, to get praise from people, or to seek happiness in something created. All that is shallow and leads to restlessness, misery, and to a bad eternity.

On the contrary, God created you for this: seeking and finding happiness in him on earth, and thus securing the glory of God in heaven. Therefore, let your heart continually say, "This one thing I do, I press on to the mark." I aim at the one purpose of my life: God. He will be my God forever and ever, and my Guide in death!

—John Wesley's sermon, "What is Man?" 1788

WHAT GOD BEGINS HE FINISHES

Being persuaded—the foundation of that persuasion we see in the following verse, "He who has begun a good work in you, will bring it to completion at the day of Jesus Christ." He has justified us; he has begun to sanctify us; he will carry on his work in us until it yields its reward in the next life.

—John Wesley, *Explanatory Notes
Upon the New Testament,* 1755

THEN! HEAVEN OPENS
IN YOUR SOUL

Eternal life begins when the Father reveals his Son in our hearts, when we first know Christ, when we call him Lord by the Holy Spirit.

Now happiness commences, happiness real, solid, substantial. Then! Heaven opens in your soul. Heaven begins while the love of God washes over your heart, instantly producing love for all. With that love comes genuine fruit: lowliness, meekness, patience, contentment in every situation, full acquiescence to the will of God—all enabling us to "rejoice evermore, and in everything to give thanks."

—John Wesley's sermon, "Spiritual Worship," 1780

THE KINGDOM OF AN
INWARD HEAVEN

s our knowledge and love of him increase, by the
same degree the kingdom of an inward heaven increases
in us. This happens while we "grow up in him who is
our Head." And when we become complete in him—
more properly, filled with him—he takes full possession
of our hearts, he reigns without a rival. That makes us
one with Christ who brings us complete happiness.

This is what the Bible means when it says, "God is
love, and whoever dwells in love, dwells in God and God
in him."

—John Wesley's sermon, "Spiritual Worship," 1780

WESLEY'S MOTHER ON THE BORDERS OF ETERNITY

I found my mother on the borders of eternity. But she had no doubt or fear; nor any desire but to depart, as soon as God called her, to be with Christ.

About three in the afternoon, I sat down on the bedside. She could not speak, but I believe she had her senses. She looked calm and serene, her eyes fixed upward, and we commended her soul to God.

Then, without struggle or sigh, her soul was set at liberty. We stood around her bed and fulfilled her last request, "Children, as soon as I am released, sing a psalm of praise to God."

* * * * *

Almost too many people to count gathered about five in the afternoon when I committed, to the earth, the body of my mother. Such a solemn assembly I seldom saw or expect to see on this side of eternity.

—John Wesley's *Journal*, July 20 and 30 and August 1, 1742

THE END OF THE WORLD

reaching in the evening at Spitalfields on "Prepare to Meet Your God," I showed the utter absurdity of
the supposition that the world would end that night.
But notwithstanding all I could say, many feared to go
to bed. Some wandered about in the fields, persuaded
that, if the world did not end, at least London would be
swallowed up by an earthquake.

I went to bed at my usual time and was fast asleep
about 10 o'clock.

—John Wesley's *Journal,* February 28, 1763

ON THE DEATH OF A FRIEND

Happy soul, your work is done,
Your fight is fought, your road is run,
   And you are now at rest:
You here were perfected in love,
You now are join'd to those above,
   And number'd with the blest.

Your sun no more goes down by night,
Your moon no more withdraws its light;
   Those blessed mansions shine
Bright with an Uncreated Flame,
Full of the glories of the Lamb,
   The eternal light Divine.

—John Wesley in *Poetics*, "After the
Death of a Friend," 1744

Week Twenty-Eight

At the same time these words
came strongly to my mind,
"These signs shall follow
those who believe."

John Wesley

MY PAIN VANISHED

I had to lie down most of the day. In the evening my weakness let up while I called sinners to repentance. But at our love feast that followed, the pain in my back and head, along with fever, continued. A cough seized me, so I could hardly speak.

At the same time, these words came strongly to my mind, "These signs shall follow those who believe." While I spoke, my pain vanished and my bodily strength returned, and for many weeks I felt neither weakness nor pain. To you, Lord, I give thanks.

—John Wesley, *Journal*, May 10, 1741

HELP!

I reminded the society that many of the brothers and sisters did not have enough food, that many did not have sufficient clothing, that others were out of work due to no fault of their own, and that many suffered illness and might die. I indicated I had done what I could to feed the hungry, clothe the naked, employ the poor, visit the sick, but that I could not, by myself, take care of all the needs. I hoped all hearts beat with my heart to help these people, so I asked them to

1. Bring what clothes each could spare and to distribute them as needed;
2. Give a penny a week, or what they could afford, for the relief of the poor and the sick.

I went on to indicate that I aimed to employ, for the present, all the women out of work in knitting.

We also appointed twelve people to visit and meet the needs of the poor. They must visit each ill person in their district every other day and meet on Tuesday evening to give an account of what they had done, and talk about what more they could do.

—John Wesley, *Journal*, May 7, 1741

A BAITED BULL!

Pensford: The place where they desired me to preach was a little green spot near the town. I had no sooner begun than a great rabble came furiously on us, bringing a bull they had baited and now tried to drive into the people. But the beast proved wiser than the drivers, and ran on one side of us or the other while we quietly sang praise to God and prayed for about an hour.

The poor wretches at length seized the bull, now weak and tired, torn and beaten by dogs and men; by sheer strength partly dragged and partly thrust him among the people. When they had forced their way to the little table on which I stood, they tried several times to throw it down by thrusting the helpless beast against it. Once or twice I pushed his head aside with my hand so the blood would not drop on my clothes. I intended to go on as soon as the hurry subsided.

But the table fell down and some of our friends caught me, then carried me away on their shoulders, while the rabble wreaked their vengeance on the table. We went a short distance where I finished preaching without noise or interruption.

—John Wesley, *Journal*, March 19, 1742

CONVERT ALL THE SCOLDS

I rode to a neighboring town to see a Justice of Peace, before whom angry neighbors had carried a whole wagon load of "new heretics." But when he asked what they had done, deep silence washed over the accusers.

At length, one said, "Why, they pretended to be better than other people; besides, they prayed from morning to night."

A Mr. Stovin asked, "But have they done nothing else?" "Yes, sir," replied an old man: "they converted my wife. Up till then, she had a terrible tongue! Now she is quiet as a lamb."

"Carry them back, carry them back," replied the justice, "and let them convert all the scolds in the town."

—John Wesley's *Journal,* June 9, 1742

QUENCH NOT THE SPIRIT

little before the service I went to Mr. Romley, the assistant minister, and offered to assist him either by preaching or reading prayers, but he did not want to use me. The church had filled with a lot of people who heard a rumor that I would preach. But the sermon, "Quench not the Spirit," did not match the expectation of many of the hearers. Mr. Romley said one of the most dangerous ways of quenching the Spirit was by getting too enthusiastic about faith. He enlarged on the character of enthusiastic believers in flowery and oratorical language.

After the sermon, John Taylor stood in the churchyard and announced to the people coming out of church that, "Mr. Wesley, not permitted to preach in the church, aims to preach here at 6 o'clock."

Well, at 6 o'clock I found such a congregation as I believe Epworth never saw before. I stood near the east end of the churchyard on my father's tombstone and cried, "The kingdom of heaven is not meat and drink; but righteousness, peace and joy in the Holy Spirit."

—John Wesley's *Journal,* June 6, 1742

LOVE'S LABOR NEVER LOST

At six I preached for the last time in Epworth churchyard to a vast multitude gathered from all parts. Our meeting went on for three hours; even then, we parted only reluctantly.

Oh! let no one think the labor of love has no fruit because it does not appear immediately. My father worked here nearly forty years, but saw little fruit from all his labor. I myself worked with these people in the past, and my energies seemed spent in vain.

But now! fruit appeared.

—John Wesley's *Journal*, June 13, 1742

POWER, LOVE, AND
A SOUND MIND

J wanted to preach in the Great Gardens lying between Whitechapel and Coverlet Fields, where I found a vast multitude gathered. Taking knowledge that a majority of them had little acquaintance with the things of God, I called upon them in the words of our Lord, "Repent and believe the gospel."

Many of the beast-like people labored a great deal to disturb those of a better mind. They threw showers of stones, one of which struck me just between the eyes, but I felt no pain.

When I had wiped away the blood, I went on testifying that God has given to them who believe "not the spirit of fear, but of power, and of love, and of a sound mind."

—John Wesley's *Journal*, September 12, 1742

Week Twenty-Nine

I am more and more convinced that the devil himself desires nothing more than that the people should be half-awakened and then left to fall asleep again. Therefore, I determine, by the grace of God, not to strike one stroke in any place where I cannot follow the blow.

John Wesley

AT TEN AT NIGHT, LESS WEARY

I began officiating at the chapel in West Street, near the Seven Dials. I preached on the Gospel for the day; afterwards I administered the Lord's Supper to some hundreds of communicants.

I became a little afraid my strength would not last, when a service of five hours (ten to three P.M.) was added to my usual schedule. But God looked after all that. I preached at the Great Gardens at five to an immense congregation on "You Must Be Born Again." Then the leaders met, and after that the small groups.

At ten in the evening, I was less weary than at six in the morning.

—John Wesley's *Journal*, May 29, 1743

HAND IN HAND

The little church in our house met together. Misunderstandings were cleared up, and we all agreed to set out anew, hand in hand, and by the grace of God, to forward one another in running the race set before us.

—John Wesley's *Journal,* February 27, 1745

BUT NOT HURT AT ALL

At Leeds, I preached at five. As we went home, a great mob followed and threw whatever came to hand. I was struck several times, once or twice in the face, but not hurt at all.

—John Wesley's *Journal*, February 22, 1746

A LITTLE GOES A LONG WAY

finished the little collection of money for helping people. It amounted to less than thirty pounds, but a few persons later made up enough to bring the total amount to fifty pounds.

By this inconsiderable sum, over two hundred fifty persons got relief in one year.

—John Wesley's *Journal*, July 17, 1746

MY PAIN CEASED

In the evening, at the chapel, my teeth pained me a great deal. Coming home, Mr. Spear told me about a serious physical problem he had had for years; he experienced a complete cure in a moment.

I prayed with submission to the will of God. My pain ceased, and it has never come back.

—John Wesley's *Journal*, November 12, 1746

WE ENTERTAIN STRANGERS

Ⅎ have not seen such a society as Tetney anywhere in England. They give to the poor. One gives eight pence, another often ten pence, and this each week. Another gives thirteen, even eighteen. Some give two shillings.

I asked Micah Elmoor, the leader, "How do you account for this? Are you the richest society in all England?"

He answered, "I do not think so, but each of us agreed to give both ourselves and *all we have* to God. We do it gladly. This accounts for the fact that from time to time we entertain strangers who come to Tetney, strangers who often have no food to eat nor a friend to give them lodging."

—John Wesley's *Journal*, February 24, 1747

PERHAPS A HUNDREDTH PART DOES NOT APPEAR

I preached in Kingwood at eight, in the afternoon at Conham, and at five in the Old Orchard to the largest congregation that I ever remember to have seen at Bristol.

What has God done in this city? Yet perhaps a hundredth part of his work does not now appear.

—John Wesley's *Journal*, August 2, 1747

Week Thirty

I strongly urged the total
giving of ourselves to God,
and renewing in every point our
covenant that the Lord
should be our God.

John Wesley

TOTAL GIVING OF OURSELVES

We met at four and solemnly rejoiced in God our Savior. I found much revival in my own soul today and so did many others.

On both this day and the following days, I strongly urged the total giving of ourselves to God, and renewing, in every point, our covenant that the Lord should be our God.

—John Wesley's *Journal*, December 25, 1747

WELL-MEANING BUT NOT QUALIFIED

At Cardiff, I spent time with T. Prosser who had filled the society with vain janglings. I found the fault lay in his head, not in his heart.

He is an honest, well-meaning man, but no more qualified, either by nature or grace, to expound Scripture than to do lectures in logic or algebra.

—John Wesley's *Journal,* September 2, 1747

EQUALLY SUSCEPTIBLE TO GOOD AND BAD

began examining the society. It had about 280 members, many of whom appeared strong in faith.

The people in general show a more teachable spirit than in most parts of England. But on that very account they must be watched with greater care, being equally susceptible to good and bad impressions.

—John Wesley's *Journal,* August 17, 1747

YOUR NAME IS LOVE

My prayer has power with God; the grace
Unspeakable I now receive;
Through faith I see you face to face;
I see you face to face, and live!
In vain I have not wept and strove—
Your nature, and your name is LOVE.

—Charles Wesley, *Hymns, and Sacred Poems,* 1742

THE EVIL OF EXAGGERATION

At Dublin, I inquired about the state of the society. I had received pompous accounts, from time to time, about the great numbers added to it. So I confidently expected to find six or seven hundred members.

But the real facts? I counted three hundred ninety-four! I doubt if there were two more than that. Let this be a warning to us not to give in to that hateful custom of painting things bigger than life. Let us make our consciences rebel against magnifying or exaggerating anything. Let us rather make understatements than overstatements.

—John Wesley's *Journal*, March 16, 1748

REAL RELIGION

cannot speak of religion without lamenting the many pretenders. So few understand what it actually means.

Authentic religion—all acquainted with it know I speak the truth—authentic believers turn their backs on mere shadows or imitations. They know by experience that true religion is the union of the soul with God, a real participation in the divine nature. It is the image of God in the soul, or to use the apostle's phrase, it is Christ formed in us. That explains why we call true religion the divine life.

—John Wesley's edition of Henry Scougal's
Life of God in the Soul of Man, 1756

GOD'S LIFE IN US

I choose to express authentic religion by the term LIFE, first because of its permanency and stability. Religion is no sudden start or passion of the mind. So many give in to the world, though they began like a shot out of a gun. They quickly withered (to change the metaphor) because they had no root in themselves.

We could compare sudden fits to the violent and convulsive movements of a beheaded chicken; however violent or impetuous, the bird cannot keep moving for very long. In contrast, the movements of holy souls show constancy and regularity, permanence and liveliness.

This divine life continues, not always in the same strength and vigor—many times it fades—yet life is not quite extinguished. Moreover, holy people do not abandon themselves to the power of corrupt affections that sway the rest of the world.

—John Wesley's edition of Henry Scougal's
Life of God in the Soul of Man, 1756

Week Thirty-One

❧

Jhad a solemn and delightful
ride to Keswick, having my
mind stayed on God.

John Wesley

RULES AT SCHOOL

rode over to Kingswood and inquired about our school there. I discovered that several of the rules had been habitually neglected, and that concerned me.

I judged it necessary, therefore, to reduce the school family, allowing no one to remain who had not decided to observe all the rules.

—John Wesley's *Journal,* July 25, 1749

WE HAVE DIFFERENT GIFTS

Mr. Whitefield preached. How wise that God gives us each different talents! Even the little improprieties, both of his language and manner, became means of profit to many who would have gone untouched by a more correct discourse, or a more calm and regular manner of public speech.

—John Wesley's *Journal,* January 28, 1750

MARKS OF GOD'S DISPLEASURE

The earthquake began about a quarter after twelve. It went through Southwark, under the river, then from one end of London to the other. People observed it at Westminster and Grosvenor Square a quarter before one.

How gently does God deal with this nation! Oh, that our repentance may prevent heavier marks of God's displeasure.

—John Wesley's *Journal*, February 8, 1750

THAT WONDERFUL PROVIDENCE

We had a comfortable watch-night service at the chapel. About eleven o'clock, I remembered that this was the very day and hour in which, forty years ago, I was taken out of the flames. I stopped, and gave a short account of that wonderful providence. The voice of praise and thanksgiving went up to heaven; great was our rejoicing before the Lord.

—John Wesley's *Journal*, February 9, 1750

Note: A lad of only six years, John Wesley nearly lost his life when ruffians set his father's rectory on fire due to the rector's uncompromising preaching. Wesley never forgot the providence that saved his life. Rescued moments before the roof collapsed, John believed he was "a brand plucked from the burning," and wanted that phrase put on his tombstone.

QUITE OVERWHELMED WITH JOY AND LOVE

At Mountmellick, Ireland, I administered the Lord's Supper to a sick person. A few of our brothers and sisters attended the occasion.

Because I had little time, I said no extemporary prayers; yet, the power of God came in such unusual power and presence during the whole time, that several did not know how to contain themselves, being quite overwhelmed with joy and love.

—John Wesley's *Journal,* April 30, 1750

PROVIDENCE AND THE COMIC

At Hull, clods and stones flew about on every side, but they neither touched nor disturbed me. When I finished my sermon, I went to take a coach, but the coachman had driven completely away.

What could we do now? Well, a gentlewoman invited my wife and me to come into her coach. She brought some inconveniences on herself by this courtesy, not only because nine of us crowded into the coach, but also because the mob followed us so closely, throwing things in at the windows (which we had to leave open for fresh air); the crowd threw anything at hand.

But a large gentlewoman who sat on my lap screened me, so that nothing came near me.

—John Wesley's *Journal*, April 24, 1752

STRENGTH FOR THE DAY

At Weardale, I had suffered illness all night and found myself now much weaker. Nonetheless, I trusted in the Strong One for my strength and began preaching to a sizable congregation.

In the evening we came to Allendale. My voice and strength now entirely restored, I cried aloud, "How shall I give you up, Ephraim?" The mountains again flowed down at his presence, and the rocks once more broke into pieces.

—John Wesley's *Journal*, May 26, 1752

Week Thirty-Two

O that in me the sacred fire
Might now begin to glow,
Burn up the dross of base desire,
And make the mountains flow!

Charles Wesley, Hymns and
Sacred Poems, *1742*

THE KING PUT ON HIS ROBES

I was in the robe-chamber adjoining the House of Lords when the king put on his robes. His brow was much furrowed with age, and quite clouded with care. Is this all the world can give even to a king?

A blanket of ermine around his shoulders, so heavy and cumbersome he can scarcely move under it! A huge heap of borrowed hair, with a few plates of gold and glittering stones on his head! Alas, what a bauble is human greatness! And even this will not endure.

—John Wesley's *Journal*, December 23, 1755

FAMILY

In the evening I met all the married men and women of the society. I believe it was high time! For many of them seemed to know very little of their family duties. So they perceived what I said strange to their ears when I enlarged on the duties of husbands and wives and parents.

—John Wesley's *Journal,* April 20, 1758

I BAPTIZED TWO NEGROES

At Wandsworth, I baptized two negroes belonging to Mr. Gilbert, a gentleman recently come from Antigua. One is deeply convinced of sin, the other rejoices in God her Savior and is the first African Christian I have known.

But the Lord, in due time, will include persons from this heathen land in his inheritance.

—John Wesley's *Journal*, November 29, 1758

Note: The language of this reading sounds foreign to our late-twentieth-century ears, ears now accustomed to racially sensitive words and phrases. But put in the context of Wesley's day, when slavery thrived, we see the evangelicals pioneering in matters of ethnic equality. John Newton (1725-1807), who led William Wilberforce to Christ, worked with Wilberforce for the abolition of slavery. John Wesley spoke out very strongly against slavery, calling it stealing and selling "our brethren like beasts." He wrote a tract called, *Thoughts on Slavery*, crying out against the evil. Wesley's very last letter was written to William Wilberforce, encouraging him in the strongest language to keep on fighting the slave trade.

WHAT A DAY OF JUBILEE!

I began reading to the society at York an account of the recent work of God at Everton. But I could not finish the reading. At first, I noticed silent tears on every side, but it was not long before several were unable to refrain from weeping aloud. Then, quickly a stout young man dropped down and cried out as if in the agonies of death. I did not attempt to read any further, but began wrestling with God in prayer.

We continued praying until almost 9:00 p.m. What a day of jubilee was this!

—John Wesley's *Journal,* July 15, 1759

THE WORK GOES ON
MORE QUIETLY

etween eight and nine I reached Everton, faint and weary enough. During the prayers, as also during the sermon and the Lord's Supper, a few persons cried aloud, not from sorrow or fear but love and joy.

I observed the same behavior in several parts of the afternoon service. In the evening two or three persons fell to the ground and were extremely convulsed, but none cried out.

I have generally observed more or less of these outward symptoms at the beginning of a general work of God. So it was in New England, Scotland, Holland, Ireland, and many parts of England, but after a time, they gradually decrease. Then the work of God goes on more quietly and silently.

—John Wesley's *Journal,* August 5 and 6, 1759

HELPING PRISONERS

I walked up to Knowle to see the French prisoners. Over 1,100 of them, confined in a small place, had nothing to lie on except dirty straw. They had nothing to cover themselves with except a few foul, thin rags (either day or night). They died like rotten sheep.

I was deeply touched and preached at Bristol in the evening on Exodus 23:9, "You shall not oppress a stranger; for you know the heart of a stranger, seeing you were strangers in the land of Egypt." The people contributed 18 pounds immediately; by the next day we had 24 pounds. With this money, we bought linen and wool cloth, made shirts out of it, also coats and pants. The people added a dozen socks.

We distributed all this carefully, giving it to prisoners with the greatest need.

—John Wesley's *Journal*, October 15, 1759

THE FLAME RAN FROM
HEART TO HEART

Many expressed surprise when I told them that the very design of a love feast* is free and familiar conversation. Anyone can speak freely to the glory of God, I answered.

Several then did speak, and not in vain. The flame ran from heart to heart, especially while one declared, with all simplicity, the manner in which God set her free during the morning sermon.

—John Wesley's *Journal,* July 19, 1761

* John Wesley revived something like the first-century Christian *agape* (love) feast, a celebration of Christ's love among believers. The symbols to this day are bread and water, and sometimes the love feast is augmented by testimony and song.

Week Thirty-Three

Father of everlasting love,
To every soul thy Son reveal,
Our guilt and suffering to remove,
Our deep, original wound to heal,
And bid the fallen race arise,
And turn our earth to paradise.

Charles Wesley, Hymns of
Intercession, *1758*

REAL LEARNING

had a good deal of conversation with John Newton. His case is very peculiar. Our church requires that clergymen be men of learning, and to this end, have a university education.

But how many have a university education and yet no learning at all? Yet these men are ordained! Meantime, one of eminent learning, as well as unblamable behavior, cannot be ordained *because he did not go to the university!*

What a mere farce this is!

—John Wesley's *Journal,* March 20, 1760

REAL CARE

hy is there not here, as in every parish in England, a special minister who takes care of all the souls? Someone here takes *charge* of all the souls; what actual *care* of them he takes is another question. It may be he neither knows nor cares whether they go to heaven or hell.

Does he ask men, women, and children any questions about their souls from one Christmas to the next? Oh! What account will such a pastor give to the Great Shepherd on Judgment Day?

—John Wesley's *Journal*, May 25, 1761

LOVE DEFINES SANCTIFICATION

o Thomas Maxfield I wrote frankly: "What I most of all dislike is your littleness of love to your brothers and sisters, your lack of meekness, gentleness and longsuffering. I also dislike your impatience with contradiction in your people. More, you look on every person as your enemy who reproves or admonishes you in love. I do not like your bigotry and narrowness of spirit."

Many years ago my brother Charles frequently said, "Your day of Pentecost has not fully come, but I do not doubt it will come. Then you will hear of persons sanctified as frequently as you now hear of persons justified." Any unprejudiced reader may observe that Pentecost has now fully come.

—John Wesley's *Journal,* November 1
and October 28, 1762

FASTING

I notice something remarkable in the way God revived his work in these parts. A few months ago, these people were terribly lacking in life.

Samuel Meggot, noticing this, advised the society to observe every Friday with fasting and prayer. The very first Friday they met together, God broke in upon them in a wonderful manner. His work has increased among them ever since.

Does the neglect of fasting account for one reason Christians go dead?

—John Wesley's *Journal*, June 7, 1763

CONNECTEDNESS

am more convinced than ever that preaching like
an apostle, without joining together those who are
awakened and training them up in the ways of God, only
gives birth to children for a murderer.

How much preaching has the whole of Pembroke-
shire heard for these twenty years! Yet they have no
regular societies, no discipline, no order or connection.
Nine out of ten of the once-awakened are now faster
asleep than ever.

—John Wesley's *Journal,* August 25, 1763

A SOLEMN CAUTION: DO NOT LOVE THE WORLD

I gave our brothers and sisters a solemn caution not to "love the world, nor the things of the world."

Herein lies their grand danger: as they apply themselves industriously and frugally, they will increase their material goods. In London, Bristol and most other trading towns, those in business increase in substance seven times, some twenty, others even a hundred times.

So you see, they need the strongest warning lest they entangle themselves in money and things, then perish.

—John Wesley's *Journal,* September 19, 1763

PERFECTING THE SAINTS

looked back to remember: Before Thomas Walsh left England, God began that great work, which has continued ever since and met with very little intermission. During the whole time many have been convinced of sin, many justified, and many backsliders healed.

But the special work, over this period of time, lies in what St. Paul calls "perfecting of the saints." Many persons in various parts of both England and Ireland have experienced so deep and universal a change that they never even conceived could be done. After a deep conviction of inbred sin, they have been so filled with faith and love—usually in a moment of time—that sin vanished, and they found from that time no pride, anger, desire or unbelief.

—John Wesley's *Journal,* November 18, 1763

Week Thirty-Four

The Spirit of God
immediately and directly
witnesses to my spirit that
I am a child of God.

John Wesley

THE WITNESS OF THE SPIRIT

The Spirit himself bears witness with our spirits that we are children of God.

—Romans 8:16

None who believe the Scriptures are the Word of God can doubt the importance of this truth, a truth revealed not once, not obscurely, not incidentally, but frequently and in very specific terms. This truth concerns Methodists, who must clearly understand, explain and defend this doctrine, because it is one grand part of the testimony God has given Methodists to communicate to all people everywhere.

By the testimony of the Spirit, I mean an inward impression on the soul, whereby the Spirit of God immediately and directly witnesses to my spirit: I am a child of God; Jesus Christ loves me; He gave himself for me; all my sins are blotted out; and I am reconciled to God.

—John Wesley's sermon, "Witness of the Spirit," 1767

THE WISDOM THAT
COMES WITH AGE

When I was much younger than I am now, I thought myself almost infallible. But I bless God that I know myself better now.

—John Wesley, *Letters*, to Lady Huntingdon, June 19, 1771

AGAINST SLAVERY

Unless the Divine Power has raised you up, I do not see how you can go through with your glorious enterprise, opposing that utterly detestable evil, the scandal of religion, of England, and of human decency. But if God stands with you, who can stand against you?

Go on in the name of God, and in the power of his might, until even American slavery, the vilest that ever saw the light of day, shall vanish completely.

—John Wesley, *Letters,* to William Wilberforce,
February 24, 1791

Note: John Wesley died six days later, March 2, 1791.

A CONSCIENCE ABOUT SPENDING

ir, I have two silver teaspoons at London, and two at Bristol. This is all the plate silver I have at present, and I will not buy any more while so many around me go hungry.

—John Wesley, *Letters,* to the Commissioner of Excise, replying to an inquiry about undeclared plate silver, September 1776

THE RELIGION OF LOVE

What does this new word, "Methodist," mean?
Does it represent a new religion? Nothing could be
further from the truth.

Methodism, so called, is the old religion, the religion
of the Bible, the religion of the early church, the religion
of the Church of England. This old religion is no other
than love, the love of God and of all persons the world
around.

—John Wesley, sermon preached on
laying the foundation of the new chapel,
City Road, London, April 21, 1777

THE POWER OF THE
SUNDAY SCHOOL

Before service, I stepped into the Bingley Sunday school of 240 children taught every Sunday by several masters and superintended by the assistant minister. So many children in one parish are restrained from open sin, instructed in a few things about good manners and taught to read the Bible.

I find these schools springing up wherever I go. Perhaps God has a deeper purpose than people are aware of.

—John Wesley's *Journal,* July 18, 1784

THE SPREAD OF THE GOSPEL

now considered how unusually the mustard seed grain of Methodism, planted about fifty years ago, has grown. It has spread through all Great Britain and Ireland; the Isle of Wight and the Isle of Man; then to America from the Leeward Islands, through the whole continent, into Canada and Newfoundland.

The societies, in all these places, have people who walk by one rule: religion makes sensible people, people who do not go around losing their temper. They also strive to worship God, not just ritualistically, but "in spirit and in truth."

—John Wesley's *Journal*, March 24, 1785

Week Thirty-Five

He or she will daily meet
with some means of drawing
nearer to God that are
unpleasing to flesh and blood.

John Wesley

SUNDAY EVENING
BEFORE DEVOTIONS

Ask these questions:

1. With what degree of attention and fervor did I pray this morning, public and private?
2. Have I done anything without at least some thought of the glory of God?
3. Did I think through what I had to do today and the spirit in which I would do it?
4. Have I done what good I could do today and done it with zeal?
5. Have I involved myself in the affairs of others beyond the bounds of charity?
6. Have I used visiting times to improve myself and others?
7. Have I gossiped?
8. Have I made today a rest day?

—John Wesley, "A Collection of Forms of Prayer for Every Day in the Week," 1733

LIVE TO THE WILL OF GOD

W̶hoever determines to live no longer to the desires of people, but to the will of God, will soon find that he or she cannot stick to that purpose without self-denial, without taking up the cross daily. That person will, every day, desire something of the world instead of the cross. But one must deny self or deny the faith. He or she will daily meet with some means of drawing nearer to God that are unpleasing to flesh and blood. In this, therefore, one must either take up the cross or renounce the Master.

—John Wesley, "A Collection of Forms of Prayer
for Every Day in the Week," 1733

SELF-DENIAL

Renounce yourself. Jesus said, If anyone wants to come after me, he or she must deny self, take up the cross and follow me. (Matthew 16:24) This implies

1. a thorough conviction that we do not belong to ourselves, that we are not the proprietors of ourselves or anything we enjoy;

2. a solemn resolution to act in line with this conviction so that we do not live for ourselves, nor pursue just our own desires, and not to act from motivations of the flesh.

—John Wesley, "A Collection of Forms of Prayer
for Every Day in the Week," 1733

I AM IN YOUR HAND

O my Father, my God, I am in your hand. May I rejoice above all things in being so. Do with me what seems good in your sight; only let me love you with all my mind, soul and strength.

—John Wesley, "A Collection of Forms of Prayer for Every Day in the Week," 1733

GRATITUDE FOR MY
CHRISTIAN BACKGROUND

𝕴 magnify you for giving me birth in your church, and for religious parents. Thank you for washing me in your baptism, instructing me in your doctrine of truth and holiness, sustaining me by your gracious providence, guiding me by your blessed Spirit. Thank you, too, for admitting me, with my Christian brothers and sisters, to wait on you in public worship, and for so often feeding my soul with your body and blood, pledges of love and strength and comfort.

Be gracious to all of us whom you admit to your holy table. Strengthen our hearts in your ways against all temptations, and make us *more than conquerors* in your love. Amen.

—John Wesley, "A Collection of Forms of Prayer
for Every Day in the Week," 1733

DELIVERANCE FROM THESE CRUEL TYRANTS

O my Father, my God, deliver me, I ask you earnestly, from all violent passions. I know these passions are greatly obstructive both to knowledge and love of you. Allow none of these out-of-control emotions to find a way into my heart, but let me always possess my soul in meekness.

O my God, I desire to fear these passions more than death. Don't let me serve these cruel tyrants; only you must reign in my heart of hearts.

Let me be your servant, yours only, and to love you with all my heart. Amen.

—John Wesley, "A Collection of Forms of Prayer for Every Day in the Week," 1733

KEEP MY PERSPECTIVE CLEAR

Deliver me, O God, from too intense an application to anything, even necessary business. I know how this dissipates my thoughts from the supreme goal of my life, and impairs that lively perception I always want to retain—seeing you stand at my right hand.

I know the narrowness of my heart, and that an eager attention to earthly things leaves no room for the things of heaven.

Teach me to go through all my work with a heart sufficiently disengaged, so that I will still see you, and perceive you always in control of my motivations, so that I will never impair that liberty of spirit that is necessary for loving you. Amen.

—John Wesley, "A Collection of Forms of Prayer
for Every Day in the Week," 1733

Week Thirty-Six

Mercifully free my heart . . .
and give me a lively, zealous, active
and cheerful spirit.

John Wesley

A FREE HEART

eliver me, O God, from a slothful mind, from all lukewarmness, and all depression of spirit. I know these cannot but deaden my love to you. Mercifully free my heart from them, and give me a lively, zealous, active and cheerful spirit, that I may vigorously perform whatever you command, thankfully suffer whatever you choose for me and be always ardent to obey your holy love in every situation. Amen.

—John Wesley, "A Collection of Forms of Prayer for Every Day in the Week," 1733

DELIVER ME FROM IDOLATROUS LOVE

Deliver me, O God, from all idolatrous love of any creature. I know a lot of people have lost you by loving creatures for their own sake, which not only permit but command love subordinate to you.

Preserve me, I ask fervently, from all such blind affection. Be my guard against all desires so that I will fix on no creature any further than the love of that which builds me up in love of you.

You require me to love you with all my heart. Help me. Be my security; in this way I will never open my heart to anything but out of love for you. Amen.

—John Wesley, "A Collection of Forms of Prayer for Every Day in the Week," 1733

ABOVE ALL FROM SELF-LOVE

bove all, deliver me, O my God, from all idolatrous self-love. I know that here lies the root of all evil. (Thank you for giving me this knowledge.)

I know you made me, not to do my own will, but yours.

I know the very corruption of the devil is a will contrary to yours.

Be my helper, against this most dangerous of all idols, so I will discern all its subtleties and withstand all its forces.

You have commanded me to renounce myself; give me strength and I will obey your command.

My real choice is to love myself, and all you have made, for you. So let your almighty arm establish, strengthen and settle me so that you will always be the ground and pillar of every bit of my love. Amen.

—John Wesley, "A Collection of Forms of Prayer
for Every Day in the Week," 1733

MY SUPREME LOVE: GOD

By love for you, my God, may my soul be fixed against its natural inconsistency; reduce me to indifference to everything but you. Give me a single desire, pleasing to you.

Let this holy flame always warm me so that I will serve you with all my might.

Let this flame burn up all selfish desires so that I will, in every situation, live first for you, not to think first of myself. Amen.

—John Wesley, "A Collection of Forms of Prayer
for Every Day in the Week," 1733

PERSONS, CHURCH, NATIONS

O my God, let your glorious name come to proper honor, loved by all you have created. Let your infinite goodness and greatness always be adored by angels and all human beings. May your church, the worldwide seminary of divine love, be protected from all the powers of darkness. Give to all who call themselves by your name one short glimpse of your goodness. May they once taste and see how gracious you are so everything else becomes tasteless.

Make them love, praise and obey you with pure, cheerful, consistent and zealous hearts, like the holy angels who worship you in heaven. Amen.

—John Wesley, "A Collection of Forms of Prayer
for Every Day in the Week," 1733

STIR UP THE NATIONS;
BLESS THE PEOPLE

Send your Spirit into the sinful nations of the world. Make a holy people. Stir up the hearts of rulers, clergy, famous people, all leaders you have put over us, that they will become happy instruments in your hand, promoting good work.

Give grace to the universities, the landowners and all who suffer. Use the trial of faith to work patience in them and perfect them in hope and love. Amen.

—John Wesley, "A Collection of Forms of Prayer
for Every Day in the Week," 1733

FAMILY, FRIENDS, ENEMIES, ME, GOD

Bless my parents, friends, relations and all who belong to my extended family. Also, bless all who serve as instruments of my good by assistance, counsel, example and writing. Help also all who do not pray for themselves.

Change the hearts of my enemies and give me grace to forgive them just as Christ forgave me.

O Shepherd of Israel, always protect me, accept my inadequate services, pardon my sins. Put a period to my sin and uneasiness, to suffering and death. Complete your church, and speed up your kingdom so we who wait for your salvation can go to heaven to love and praise you forever. In the name of God the Father, God the Son, and God the Holy Ghost, throughout all ages, world without end. Amen.

—John Wesley, "A Collection of Forms of Prayer
for Every Day in the Week," 1733

Week Thirty-Seven

Do I think of God first and last? How have I behaved since I went to bed last night? Have I resolved to do all the good I can today and to follow through on my calling with all diligence?

John Wesley

PRAISE TO GOD

God, Giver of all good gifts, I want to praise your name for all the expressions of your bounty toward me. Thank you for your love in giving your Son to die for my sins, for the means of grace, for hope.

Thank you for your love for all temporal benefits which you give with a liberal hand poured out on me: my health and strength, food and clothes, all necessities.

I also want to thank you that even after all my refusals of your grace, you still have patience with me. You preserved me through the night and gave me a new day. You complete my repentance. Amen.

—John Wesley, "A Collection of Forms of Prayer
for Every Day in the Week," 1733

FAITHFUL SERVANTS ALL

xtend, I humbly ask, your mercy to all people. Make us all faithful servants.

Help all Christians to live up to their profession. Make sinful nations good. Reform us but not by destruction.

Turn us around. Show us favor. Give us grace to put a period to our ways of provoking people to sin. Do put a stop to our punishment.

Defend our church from splits, heresy, and efforts to destroy the sense of the sacred. Bless all bishops, pastors, and church workers; give them the graces of the apostles; make them examples; help them to teach sound doctrine.

Keep our national leaders from all deceptions and manipulations. Grant them your wisdom, integrity and zeal. Give to the universities quietness and industry. Amen.

—John Wesley, "A Collection of Forms of Prayer
for Every Day in the Week," 1733

SELF-EXAMINATION:
1. SINGLE-MINDEDNESS

Am I single-minded in thought and deed? Do I see God as my good, my pattern, my one desire? Do I act only for him? Does he determine the parameters of my views and behavior every hour? In order to do this, have I kept faith with my accountability group? Do I do anything I do not perceive as the will of God? Or anything that does not contribute to making my days better? Does my speech reflect godly intentions?

—John Wesley, "A Scheme of Self-Examination,"
Used by the first Methodists in Oxford, 1791

SELF-EXAMINATION:
2. FERVENT PRAYER

Have I prayed with fervor? When I go to church? Morning and evening? With my friends? In all I do at work? For help when I'm a leader of worship?

Do I attend worship regularly whenever possible? Do I spend adequate time in daily private prayer? Do I stop myself in these private prayers, now and then, to ask if I maintain the inner glow? Do I make my prayers my own? Do I conclude in his name, the name of the One who intercedes for me at the right hand of God?

—John Wesley, "A Scheme of Self-Examination,"
Used by the first Methodists in Oxford, 1791

SELF-EXAMINATION:
3. GOOD WORKS

m I zealous to do good works? Do I embrace every opportunity of doing good and preventing, removing or lessening evil? Do I pursue good works with all my power?

Do I hold anything too dear to part with to serve my neighbor?

—John Wesley, "A Scheme of Self-Examination,"
Used by the first Methodists in Oxford, 1791

SELF-EXAMINATION: 4. SPEECH

Do I spend adequate time talking to people? Do I patiently work with people as long as they let me? Do I learn, insofar as possible and before talking, about their emotional make-up, way of thinking, past life, hindrances? Do I size up motives and difficulties, then in balanced perspective exhort them to think calmly and deeply and pray earnestly?

When I speak to strangers, do I indicate what religion is not (it is not negative, it is not external), and what it is (a recovery of the image of God)? Do I try to discover at what step strangers have come to and what made them stop in their search?

Do I persuade all I can to attend public prayers, sermons and sacraments? And to obey the laws of the church, state and school?

Do I argue with grace? Do I speak with reserve?

Do I rejoice with my neighbor in celebration and grieve in his or her pain? Do I listen to my neighbor's problems with empathy and not anger?

Do I speak unkindly about or to my neighbor? Do I reveal any evil about anyone, unless absolutely necessary for some good? Do I make such revelations in tenderness and consistency? Do I ever approve of gossip?

Does good will constitute the springboard of all my actions toward others?

Do I pray for people after speaking to them? For my students? For those who have asked for prayer? For my family every day?

—John Wesley, "A Scheme of Self-Examination,"
Used by the first Methodists in Oxford, 1791

HOW TO DO
SPIRITUAL READING

First, set aside a time each day. Observe it, so far as possible, as a sacred duty.

Second, prepare yourself for reading by purity of intention. Aim at the good of your soul by fervent prayer, so you can see his will and get from him a firm resolution to do it.

Third, read not out of curiosity or hastily, but leisurely, seriously and with great intention. Pause from time to time, inviting enlightenings of divine grace. Read in sequence, not here and there, to the end of the book.

Fourth, identify with what you read so that in addition to the enlightenment of your understanding, your emotions engage with the material. Lift up prayers here and there as you read. Tuck special treasures away in your heart against the day of temptations and crises.

Finally, ask God both to plant and bring to flower the seed sown in your heart.

—John Wesley, "A Scheme of Self-Examination,"
Used by the first Methodists in Oxford, 1791

Week Thirty-Eight

Watch and pray continually against pride.

John Wesley

THE LIGHT OF JESUS

Send down your likeness from above,
    And let this my adorning be:
Clothe me with wisdom, patience, love,
    With lowliness and purity,
Than gold and pearls more precious far,
And brighter than the morning star.

Lord, arm me with your Spirit's might,
    Since I am call'd by your great name:
In you my wandering thoughts unite,
    Of all my works be you the aim.
Your love attend me all my days,
And my sole business be your praise!

—John Wesley's translation from the German
of Joachim Lange (1670-1744)

SUBTLE PRIDE!

Watch and pray continually against pride. If God has cast it out, see that it never enters again. Its danger parallels evil desire.

You may slide back into pride unawares, especially if you think there is no danger of its returning.

To say, "I give God all the credit," can itself be pride. Pride expresses itself not only when we give credit to ourselves, but when we think we have something we do not. Mr. L., for instance, ascribed all the light he had to God, and in that he demonstrated humility. But then he thought he had more light than any person living— that's pride!

—John Wesley, *A Plain Account of Christian Perfection*, 1777

THE UNCOMMON
JOHN FLETCHER

I find peculiar difficulty giving a full account of either the life or character of John Fletcher. He gave us very little light about himself. On all occasions, he showed uncommon reserve in speaking about himself, both in writing and conversation.

He seldom referred to himself unless it slipped from him unawares. And among the many papers he left, hardly a page (except a single account of his conversion to God) relates either to his own inward experience or the transactions of his life. So most of the information we have comes from short hints scattered up and down in his letters or from what he dropped among his friends. We do get some help from what people remember about him.

—John Wesley, "A Short Account of the Life and Death
of the Reverend John Fletcher," 1786

HOW TO RECEIVE ADVICE

Do not say to any who would advise or reprove you, "You are blind; you cannot teach me." And do not say, "This is just your own wisdom, your carnal reason." But calmly weigh what you hear before God.

—John Wesley, *A Plain Account of Christian Perfection*, 1777

ADMIT YOUR FAULTS

Always stand ready to own any fault. If you have at any time thought, spoken or acted wrongly, do not hesitate to acknowledge it.

Never so much as dream that acknowledgment will hurt the cause of God; no, it will only further it!

Therefore, talk openly and frankly when burdened by something you did. Do not try to evade or disguise it. Rather, tell it like it is, and you will not hinder but adorn the gospel.

—John Wesley, *A Plain Account of Christian Perfection*, 1777

RADICALISM

Beware of that daughter of pride, radicalism. Oh! keep at the utmost distance from it. Give no place to an overcharged imagination. Do not hastily ascribe things to God. Do not easily suppose dreams, voices, impressions, visions or revelations come from God. They may come from him; they may come from nature; they may come from the devil.

Therefore, "do not believe every spirit, but test the spirits to see if they come from God." Test everything by the written Word and submit to its authority. You place yourself in danger every hour if you depart even a little from Scripture. Just let the text, in its plain meaning seen within its context, serve as your standard. Reason, knowledge and human learning, good as they are, must submit to the Bible.

—John Wesley, *A Plain Account of Christian Perfection,* 1777

THE SUPREME GIFT: LOVE

major reason for a thousand mistakes relates to avoiding love, the highest gift of God. Humble, gentle, patient love. All visions, revelations, manifestations reduce to small things compared to love.

Make yourself thoroughly alive to this truth: the heaven of heavens is love. Religion offers nothing higher than this. In effect, there is nothing else but love.

If you look for anything but more love, you look wide of the mark. you search outside the royal way.

When you ask others, "Have you received this or that blessing?" if you mean anything but more love, you mean wrong. You lead them astray and put them onto a false scent.

Settle it then in your heart that from the moment God saved you from sin, your aim can only spell LOVE described in I Corinthians 13. You can go no higher than this until you reach heaven.

—John Wesley, *A Plain Account of Christian Perfection,* 1777

Week Thirty-Nine

Give to the winds your fears,
Hope and be undismay'd;
God hears your sighs,
and counts your tears,
God shall lift up your head.

John Wesley

GIVE TO THE WIND
YOUR FEARS

Give to the winds your fears,
Hope, and be undismay'd;
God hears your sighs, and counts your tears,
God shall lift up your head.

Through waves and clouds and storms
He gently clears your way;
Wait now his time, so shall this night
Soon end in joyous day.

Still heavy is your heart?
Still sink your spirits down?
Cast off the weight, let fear depart,
And every care be gone.

Leave to his sovereign sway
To choose and to command;
So shall you wondering own, his way
How wise, how strong his hand.

Far, far above your thought
His counsel shall appear,
When fully he the work has wrought
That caused you needless fear.

Let us in life, in death,
Your steadfast truth declare,
And publish with our latest breath
Your love and guardian care!

—John Wesley's translation from the German
of Paulus Gerhardt (1607-1676)

A TRUE MARRIAGE

John Fletcher did not willingly, much less by design, conceal anything from his wife. They had no secrets with regard to each other, but had one house, one purse, one heart.

In her presence he invariably thought aloud, always opening a window in his heart.

—John Wesley, "A Short Account of the Life and
Death of the Reverend John Fletcher," 1786

STEADY RELIANCE

John Fletcher did not allow sights or impressions (which many mistake for faith) to lead him, but a steady, firm reliance on the love and truth and faithfulness of God. His ardent desire rested in belief strong enough to make him a partaker of the great promises and to be a witness to the mind of Christ Jesus.

Conscious that he must go to the cross with the Master or never reign with him, he gave his life to him. He saw himself as clay in his hand.

He often said, "In all events I must hang on the Lord with a sure trust and confidence that he will order all things in the best time and manner. If I could see everything, how could I have faith? But against hope I believe in hope, because of the Unseen Power that mightily supports us in all our dangers and difficulties—that belief God accepts."

Sometimes when I have expressed apprehension of an upcoming trial, he would say, "I do not doubt the Lord orders everything; therefore, I leave all to him." He seemed to show no fear, even in great dangers.

John Fletcher said, "I know God always gives his angels charge of us. Therefore we are equally safe everywhere."

—John Wesley quoting Mrs. Fletcher in
"A Short Account of the Life and Death
of the Reverend John Fletcher," 1786

PATIENCE

Patience produced in John Fletcher a mind that embraced every cross with readiness and pleasure. For the good of his neighbors, nothing seemed hard, nothing wearisome.

Sometimes I have hesitated to call him out of his study two or three times in an hour, especially when writing some of his deep works. But John Fletcher always responded positively: "O my dear, never think of that. It does not matter, if we always stand ready to do the will of God. Conformity to his will alone makes work excellent."

He never thought anything too common, but sin; he never saw anything as beneath him. If he overtook a poor man or woman on the road with a burden too heavy, he did not fail to offer help. He would not take no easily.

—John Wesley quoting Mrs. Fletcher in
"A Short Account of the Life and Death
of the Reverend John Fletcher," 1786

PAIN AND COURAGE

John Fletcher bore pain in a most exemplary way, growing through suffering more and more to the last.

Moreover, he did not get upset with ignorant people. He knew how to come to the level of anyone.

Yet he faced sin with resolute courage, reproving it forthrightly. To daring sinners he was a son of thunder. And he refused to allow the influence of the world to hinder his condemnation of sin, when he believed God gave him a message to deliver to offending people.

—John Wesley quoting Mrs. Fletcher in
"A Short Account of the Life and Death
of the Reverend John Fletcher," 1786

KNOW YOURSELF

John Fletcher knew his place and stood firm in it. Every person has his or her special assignment in the human race, an assignment made by the wise Masterbuilder. All goes well so long as one sticks to that assignment.

But as every dislocated bone gives pain, until replaced to its proper place, so every dislocated desire must give pain to the soul until restored to its own place.

Whatever John believed was the will of God, he resolutely did, even if that meant taking out an eye or laying Isaac on the altar. When God called John to go some place, he immediately prepared for the journey without hesitation. He went, despite his last years of life when he seldom traveled any considerable distance without feeling he might relapse into a disease he once suffered, and usually some weeks passed before he recovered his usual strength.

—John Wesley quoting Mrs. Fletcher in
"A Short Account of the Life and Death
of the Reverend John Fletcher," 1786

HUSBAND AND WIFE
DEDICATED TOGETHER

John Fletcher never went into debt. He gave away all he could and lived by a rule to pay money on the spot for every purchase; this kept his mind unencumbered and free of care.

Meanwhile, his substance, time and strength, his very life, he devoted to the service of the poor.

He even gave me to the poor! When we married, he asked about my willingness to "marry his parish." The first time he took me among his people, he said, "I have not married this wife only for myself but for you. I asked her for your comfort as well as my own."

—John Wesley quoting Mrs. Fletcher in
"A Short Account of the Life and Death
of the Reverend John Fletcher," 1786

Week Forty

Lo, God is here!
Him day and night
The united choirs of angels sing.

John Wesley

GOD'S PRESENCE

Lo, God is here! Let us adore
   And own how awesome is this place!
Let all within us feel his power,
   And silent bow before his face,
Who know his power, his grace who prove,
Serve him with awe, with reverence love.

Lo, God is here! Him day and night
   The united choirs of angels sing:
To him enthroned above all height
   Heaven's hosts their noblest praises bring:
Disdain not, Lord, our meaner song,
Who praise you with a stammering tongue.

Being of beings, may our praise
   Your courts with grateful fragrance fill;
Still may we stand before your face,
   Still hear and do your sovereign will.
To you may all our thoughts arise,
Ceaseless, accepted sacrifice!

           —John Wesley's translation from the German of
                Gerhard Tersteegen (1697-1769)

BEWARE OF CHURCH SPLITS

Beware of schism, of making a split in the church of Christ. Do not allow disunion. When members cease to have love "one for another" (I Cor. 12:25), they expose the root of all contention. Beware of a dividing spirit; shun any hint of it.

So do not say, "I am of Paul or of Apollos," the very thing that separated the church at Corinth. Do not say, "This is my preacher; the best preacher in England. Give me him and you can have the others." All this breeds division; it separates those God has joined.

Do not despise or run down any preacher; do not exalt any one above the rest, for you might hurt both preacher and God's cause.

Do not come down hard on any preacher because of incoherent speech, inaccuracy of expression, or mistakes of any kind.

Rather, talk about what God has done for you, especially his gift of love for people everywhere.

—John Wesley, *A Plain Account of Christian Perfection*, 1777

PRAISE FOR THE GRACE
OF AFFLICTIONS

The bottom of your soul may lie in peace even while you suffer many outward troubles, just as the bottom of the sea stays calm while the surface is strongly agitated.

The best helps to growth in grace come when we suffer affronts and losses. We should receive them with all thankfulness, as preferable to everything else, if for no other reason than that we willed no part of the afflictions.

The quickest way to escape from your sufferings lies in willingness to endure them so long as God pleases. To put up with persecution and suffering with a right attitude means you attain a higher measure of conformity to Christ.

What is one of the greatest evidences of God's love? Afflictions with grace to bear them. One of the ways God draws people closer to himself relates to affliction about something dearly loved or from some good action done with an eye focused on God's glory. Nothing can show us so vividly the emptiness of even the most lovely and desirable things the world offers.

—John Wesley, *A Plain Account of Christian Perfection*, 1777

IN PRAISE OF LOVE
IN TOUGH TIMES

I am glad you have learned to say, "The Lord gives and the Lords takes away." Your child has gone, but only a little while before you get to heaven. Time flies; how soon you will overtake her! In no way is it inconsistent with Christian resignation to request conditionally, "Let this cup pass from me," because you follow with the additional comment, "Nevertheless, not as I will, but as you will."

Rapturous joy, frequently given in the beginning days of justification or entire sanctification, comes as a great blessing. But it seldom continues long before it subsides into calm, peaceful love.

—John Wesley, *Letters,* to Mrs. Barton, July 29, 1777

GRATITUDE FOR THE
JOY TO COME

When the Son of Man comes in glory and assigns everyone to his or her own reward, that reward will undoubtedly be proportioned first, to our inward holiness or likeness to God, second, to our works, and third to our sufferings. So for whatever you suffer in time, you will gain in eternity.

Many of your sufferings, perhaps the greatest part, you have put behind you. But the joy will come! Look up, dear friend, look up to see the crown before you! A little longer and you will drink of the rivers of pleasure that flow at God's right hand for evermore.

—John Wesley, *Letters*, to Ann Bolton, December 15, 1786

MY STRENGTH, MY JOY,
MY CROWN

You will I love, my strength, my tower;
   You will I love, my joy, my crown;
You will I love with all my power,
   In all my works, and you alone!
You will I love, till the pure fire
Fills my whole soul with chaste desire.

—John Wesley's translation from the German
of Johann Scheffler (1624-1677)

HEALED MY WOUNDED MIND

I thank you, Uncreated Sun,
    That your bright beams on me have shined;
I thank you, who have overthrown
    My foes, and heal'd my wounded mind;
I thank you, whose enlivening voice
Bids my freed heart in you rejoice.

Uphold me, in the doubtful race,
    Nor allow me again to stray;
Strengthen my feet, with steady pace
    Still to press forward in your way;
My soul and flesh, O Lord of Might,
Fill, saturate with your heavenly light.

—John Wesley's translation from the German
of Johann Scheffler (1624–1677)

Week Forty-One

❧

The essential part of Christian
holiness lies in giving your
heart wholly to God.

John Wesley

THE ESSENTIAL OF
CHRISTIAN HOLINESS

When we love one another, we have no need of either disguise or reserve. I love you and I truly believe you love me, so you need write only just what you feel.

The essential part of Christian holiness lies in giving your heart wholly to God. Your present need is not to reason out what to call your experience, but to go straight to him who loves you, with all your wants, great or small. God will give you the help you need.

You have only to receive his help by simple faith. Nevertheless, you will always live with numberless infirmities because you live in a house of clay. So this corruptible body will more or less press down on the soul; yet, not so as to prevent your joy and witness that your heart belongs one hundred percent to him.

You may claim this; it belongs to you because Christ belongs to you. Believe and sense him near.

—John Wesley, *Letters*, to Mrs. Bennis, July 25, 1767

ALL GOOD BRANCHES OUT
FROM LOVE

The ability to put your mind on one matter, to employ the whole vigor of your mind on a single focus, may result in excellent achievements. But you do need to be on your guard to make sure you aim at a good goal. More, make sure your goal leads you to the best, not the second best. Then whatever your hand finds to do, do it with your might.

What is your chief goal? To walk in love as Christ loved us and gave himself for us. Humble, gentle, patient love wraps up every good goal. To know this assists us to overcome the narrowness of our minds and the scantiness of our understanding. Every right emotion, and therefore all right words and actions, naturally branch out of love.

So you see that you have no other need but this—to be filled with the faith that works by love.

—John Wesley, *Letters*, to Philothea Briggs, January 5, 1772

A DEVOTED WILL

A will, steadily and evenly devoted to God, is essential to sanctification, but not to a consistency of joy or peace or happy communion with God. These may rise and fall in various degrees due to the condition of your body or an evil cause. All our wisdom cannot understand or prevent these ups and downs.

Go straight to God like a little child; tell him all your troubles, hindrances and doubts, and let him know you want all your problems turned into good.

In sending you to Waterford, God expects you to do good. Stir up the gift of God in you; gather the scattered ones; make a group or two. Visit from house to house; in this way you will see how the people live. Talk to the young in the families. By this kind of activity, you will get warm friendliness in return; by imparting life you will increase it in yourself.

Take up your cross; bear it and it will bear you.

—John Wesley, *Letters*, to Mrs. Bennis, January 18, 1774

A SECRET OF FAITH DEVELOPMENT

Have a single focus, a steady design, to build people up by good works. To do this, we must have help from heaven. God's help will enable us to order our conversations rightly to help both others and our own souls.

Before you can help people effectively, you must conquer your natural reserve by taking initiative with people you know not at all or very little.

Do not go out less but more. Use your increased faith and love or it will fade and die. Only by doing good works can you perfect your faith.

The more you love solitude and engage in it, the more it will increase. This temptation is common to people everywhere. Satan says, "To the desert!" I say, "To the Bible!" And in the Bible we learn that as you have time, do good to all, warn and encourage.

—John Wesley, *Letters*, to Mary Bishop, November 30, 1774

GOD'S PRESENCE ALL THE TIME

Though I am always in haste, I am never in a hurry. I never take more work than I can go through with perfect calmness of spirit. True, I travel four or five thousand miles a year. But generally I travel in my carriage and consequently retire ten hours a day, as if alone in a wilderness. Few spend so many hours secluded from people. Yet I find time to visit the sick and the poor; indeed, I must do that if I believe the Bible, which tells us these marks will identify us to the Shepherd of Israel at the Great Day.

When I lived at Oxford, almost like a hermit, I could not understand how busy people could have salvation. I could hardly see how busy people retain the Christian spirit in the midst of noise and bustle in the world. God taught me better by my own experience. I had ten times more work in America than I ever had before. But my schedule in no way hindered the calm in me.

Mr. Boehm served as chaplain and secretary to Prince George of Denmark, secretary to Queen Anne, and was manager of almost all the public charities in the kingdom. He also had many personal duties. An intimate friend once asked him, "Sir, doesn't this amazing hurry and work hurt you? I have seen you in your office surrounded by people; you listen, dictate, write—in all that, can you retain a sense of the presence of God?"

He answered: "All that company and business no more hinders or lessens my communion with God than if I knelt all alone in a church at the communion table."

So do not be a hermit in Mexico. Do not content yourself with lower degrees of usefulness and holiness.

—John Wesley, *Letters*, to Miss March, December 10, 1777

I CORINTHIANS 13

advised Jenny Cooper and I advise you to read often and meditate on I Corinthians 13. There you see the true picture of Christian perfection! Copy those admonitions with all your might. Read too, more than once, my *Plain Account of Christian Perfection.*

Christian perfection is nothing more than humble, gentle, patient love! Undoubtedly, we have the privilege to rejoice always calm, still, heartfelt joy. But we seldom experience this continuously; many circumstances make rejoicing ebb and flow, so this cannot be the essence of religion. The essence of religion is humble, gentle, patient love.

Can we wrap up all this in the word *resignation?* Yes, because the highest lesson our Lord, as a man, learned on earth was to say, "Not as I will, but as you will." Ask God to conform you to his will more and more.

—John Wesley, *Letters,* to Ann Loxdale, April 12, 1782

INWARD RELIGION

Author of faith, eternal Word,
  Whose Spirit breathes the active flame;
Faith, like its finisher and Lord,
  Today as yesterday the same.

To you our humble hearts aspire
  And ask the gift unspeakable;
Increase in us the kindled fire,
  In us the work of faith fulfill.

Faith lends its realizing light,
  The clouds disperse, the shadows fly;
Th'Invisible appears in sight,
And God is seen by mortal eye.

—John Wesley, *Hymns and Sacred Poems*, 1740

Week Forty-Two

Every new victory a soul
gains comes as the result of prayer.

John Wesley

NOTHING COMES EXCEPT
BY PRAYER

God seldom gives his Spirit, even to those he has established in grace, if they do not pray for it on all occasions; not only once, but many times.

God does nothing except in answer to prayer. Even those converted without praying for new birth—exceedingly rare—do not come into the kingdom without others praying for them.

Every new victory a soul gains comes as the effect of prayer.

—John Wesley, *A Plain Account of Christian Perfection,* 1777

PRAYER IN CRISIS

Whenever crisis comes, go to prayer so you will open the door to grace and light from God. Then make your decision. This procedure robs you of despair about whether or not the decision will succeed.

—John Wesley, *A Plain Account of Christian Perfection*, 1777

PRAYER IN TEMPTATION

In the greatest temptations, a single look at Christ, even barely saying his name, does the job of overcoming the wicked one, just so long as you say his name with confidence and calmness of spirit.

—John Wesley, *A Plain Account of Christian Perfection*, 1777

"PRAY WITHOUT CEASING"

God's command to "pray without ceasing" is founded on the necessity of his grace to preserve the life of God in our souls. Our souls can no more continue one moment without the life of God than the body can live without air.

Whether we think about God, or talk to him, or act for him, or suffer for him—all is prayer when we live for no other object than his love, and the desire to please him.

All a Christian does—even eating and sleeping— becomes prayer when lived out as prayer and when done in simplicity, with singular purpose.

—John Wesley, *A Plain Account of Christian Perfection,* 1777

WHAT MOTIVATES CONTINUOUS PRAYER?

Prayer continues because of the desires of our hearts. In souls filled with love, the desire to please God is a continual prayer. This strong love we can call "crying after God."

God requires of his adult children only that their hearts reveal themselves to him as genuinely purified; also that they offer him continually the wishes and promises that naturally spring from perfect love.

These desires, the genuine fruits of love, are the most perfect prayers.

—John Wesley, *A Plain Account of Christian Perfection,* 1777

KEEP YOUR HEART PURE

As a particle of dust will disorder a clock, and the slightest bit of sand will obscure our sight, so the least grain of sin in the heart will hinder its right movement toward God.

—John Wesley, *A Plain Account of Christian Perfection,* 1777

PRAYER IN CHURCH AND HOME

Live in the church as saints live in heaven. Live in your house as the holiest of people live in the church. Do your house work with the same sincerity you pray in church.

Worship God from the very bottom of your heart.

—John Wesley, *A Plain Account of Christian Perfection,* 1777

Week Forty-Three

The best way to resist the devil is to destroy whatever of the world remains in us.

John Wesley

RESIST AND GROW

ontinually labor to cut off all the useless things that surround us, i.e., the superfluities of our souls. God will help us.

The best means of resisting the devil is to destroy the world remaining in us. In this way, we will make for God a building constructed of love.

Just then we begin, in this quickly passing life, to love God as we shall love him in eternity.

—John Wesley, *A Plain Account of Christian Perfection*, 1777

DANGEROUS WINDS

As dangerous winds enter at little openings, so the devil enters most dangerously by little, unobserved incidents. Those incidents seem nothing, yet unknowingly they open hearts to great temptations.

Therefore, renew yourself from time to time, closely examining the state of your soul. Do it as if you never did it before. Nothing encourages the full assurance of faith more than keeping yourself by this means of humility, and by the exercise of all the good works you do.

—John Wesley, *A Plain Account of Christian Perfection,* 1777

VIGILANCE

If, after renouncing the world, we do not watch incessantly, and fervently ask God to accompany our vigilance with his vigilance, we will get entangled and the world will overcome us.

To continual watchfulness and prayer we must add continual work. For grace flies away from a vacuum, and the devil fills whatever God does not fill.

—John Wesley, *A Plain Account of Christian Perfection*, 1777

SPIRITUAL DIRECTION

spiritual director and a person being guided must exercise real faithfulness. They must continually regard each other as God would, examine themselves to insure pure thoughts and make sure all their words show Christian discretion.

Other affairs are only the things of the world, but these affairs are peculiarly the things of God.

—John Wesley, *A Plain Account of Christian Perfection*, 1777

A PRINCIPLE RULE

One of the principal rules of religion, we can state like this: *miss no opportunity to serve God.* We cannot see God, but we can see our neighbor. When we serve our neighbor, we serve God; in this way people can see his work.

God perceives that work as done for himself in the flesh, as if he stood visibly before us. Constant attention to the work, with which God intrusts us, is a mark of solid piety.

—John Wesley, *A Plain Account of Christian Perfection,* 1777

TONGUE, HANDS, HEART

St. Paul says no one can call Jesus, "Lord," except by the help of the Holy Spirit. Those words show us the necessity of seeing God in our good works, and even in our small thoughts. No act or thought pleases him more than those he forms in us and with us.

That means we cannot serve him unless he has liberty to use our tongue, hands and heart in the way he wants to.

If we could do good things on our own, we could give ourselves credit; but, we have to have his help. That's why he gets credit; the good works come from his grace. That makes the works divine and explains why he honors himself in us through those good efforts.

—John Wesley, *A Plain Account of Christian Perfection,* 1777

WHAT IS GREATNESS?

God is so great that he communicates greatness for the least thing done in his service. If one gets sick, or even dies, by doing good works, one can count him or herself happy.

God frequently conceals the part his children play in the conversion of souls. Yet one may boldly say that the one who prays fervently over a long period of time for the conversion of someone—that prayer has played a significant role in the conversion.

—John Wesley, *A Plain Account of Christian Perfection,* 1777

Week Forty-Four

The kingdom of God is
righteousness, peace and
joy in the Holy Spirit. It is holiness
and happiness.

John Wesley

HOW TO ENTER THE KINGDOM OF GOD

A sinner, drawn out by the love of the Father, enlightened by the Son ("the true light that lights every person who comes into the world"), convicted of sin by the Holy Spirit—that person comes heavy with sin and casts all sins on him, the One "mighty to save."

He or she then receives from him true, living faith. Put right by that faith, my spirit knows peace with God, which now rules. One also rejoices in the hope of God's glory. The newly converted one knows that sin has no more power over him or her.

Love now captures the heart and produces holy motivations and good conversation.

> —John Wesley's edition of "An Account of the
> Life and Death of Dr. Barnes" (extracted
> from the *Book of Martyrs*), 1739

BACKSLIDING

great servant of God, Dr. Barnes, at times fell back from the glorious liberty that freed him from fear, sin and bondage. Why? Because God lost his power? Certainly not. It is because Barnes did not live in Christ, because he did not grasp him with all his heart, and because he grieved the Holy Spirit who had sealed the work of grace. He may have slid back unconsciously. When the Spirit leaves us for a time, we become weak like others.

But God shows mercy to us with our infirmities, follies and sins. God promises he will be mindful of us. Oh, let us be so of him!

—John Wesley's edition of "An Account of the
Life and Death of Dr. Barnes" (extracted
from the *Book of Martyrs*), 1739

MAKE CHRISTIANS, NOT PARROTS

I ask you in earnest to think through carefully how you teach your children about the deep things of God. Beware of that common but bad way of making children parrots instead of Christians. Work at helping them understand every sentence they read. Don't hurry. Don't aim at covering a great deal, but at how well and for what good purpose they read.

Turn each sentence every way. Look at it in every light. Question it on every point. In this way, you will do your part to help them inwardly digest, not just read, the words of eternal life.

—John Wesley, "Lessons for Children," Part I, 1746

TO ALL PARENTS
AND TEACHERS

Instill true principles of Christian education in
your children as early in life as possible. If the fear of the
Lord is the beginning of wisdom, surely it is the very
first truth they should learn. Teach them the knowledge
of God along with their other studies.

Let the truths you will teach engrave themselves
deeply into your own heart. Then you will spare no
pains in teaching these truths.

Do not let the children read a single line without
understanding what they read. Have them repeat sen-
tences over and again; talk about them, and say what
they mean. Work with the children until each truth
really takes hold of them. In this way, they will learn to
think as they learn to read; they will grow wiser and
better every day. And you will have the reward of watching them grow in grace, in the knowledge of God and of
our Lord Jesus Christ.

—John Wesley, "Lessons for Children," Part II, 1747

THE RICH RESOURCE IN BOOKS

We are blessed to have a great variety of books in English on every branch of religion. This variety is abundantly increased, especially in our day. We are enriched even more by translations from other languages, ancient as well as modern.

So even to spend forty years in untiring effort, one could only go a little way toward reading the published works of our own tongue, works published in the last 150 years.

—John Wesley's Preface to *A Christian Library,* 1749

MY HEART'S DESIRE FOR YOU

My heart's desire and prayer to God for you is that you may never rest short of this: Phillipians 4:8, "Finally, brethren, whatever is true, whatever is honorable, whatever is just, whatever is pure, whatever is lovely, whatever is gracious, if there is any excellence, if there is anything worthy of praise, think about these things" [RSV]. "But my God shall supply all your need, according to his riches in glory by Christ Jesus" [v. 19, KJV].

—John Wesley, *Letters,* to the Countess
of Hungingdon, August 1744

IN PRAISE TO GOD

Thou neither can be felt or seen;
    You are a Spirit pure,
Who from eternity has been,
    And always shall endure.

Whate'er you will in earth below,
    You do in heaven above:
But chiefly we rejoice to know
    Th'almighty God is Love.

—John Wesley, *Hymns for Children and Others
of Riper Years*, 1768 (2d edition)

Note: John Wesley did not have the benefit of human development studies. What strikes us is his interest in little ones in a day when the culture said children should be seen and not heard.

Week Forty-Five

❧

The one who burns with love for all humankind, who neither thinks, speaks nor acts but to fulfill God's will—that person is on the last round of the ladder to heaven.

John Wesley

THE LAST ROUND OF THE LADDER TO HEAVEN

Christ lives in me—just there we have the fulfilling of the law, the last stage of Christian holiness. This defines perfection. It refers to the Christian, dead to the world and alive to God; the one whose only desire relates to God's name.

Here we see a person who has given the total heart to God, who delights in him, and in nothing else but what he intends.

Such a person burns with love for all humankind, who neither thinks, speaks nor acts, but to fulfill God's will—that person is on the last round of the ladder to heaven; grace has had its full work in the soul. The next steps takes one into glory.

—John Wesley, *A Collection of Forms of Prayer for Every Day in the Week*, 1738

A PRAYER TO BE LIKE CHRIST

May the God of glory give us, who have not already become like Christ, the grace to forget those things that lie behind us, and reach to those things that lie before us, to press toward the mark for the prize of our high calling in Christ Jesus. Amen.

—John Wesley, *A Collection of Forms of Prayer for Every Day in the Week*, 1738

A PRAYER FOR ENLIGHTENMENT

May God so enlighten our eyes that we may count all things loss for the excellency of the knowledge of Christ Jesus our Lord; and in this way establish our hearts that we may rejoice to endure the loss of all things, and count them but refuse so we may win Christ. Amen.

—John Wesley, *A Collection of Forms of Prayer for Every Day in the Week,* 1738

A PRAYER OF KNOWING

Lord, I know you have commanded me, and therefore it is my duty, to love you with all my heart and all my strength.

O Lord, I know you created me and that I have neither life nor happiness unless you give them by your power and goodness.

O Lord, I know you are the purpose of my life, and that I can expect no happiness, except in you.

O Lord, I know that to me, lost in sin, you sent your only Son out of love; that he, though Lord of glory, humbled himself to die on a cross that I might be raised to glory.

O Lord, I know you provide me with all necessary helps for carrying me through this life to that eternal glory; you make this provision out of your mercy to me, though I do not stand worthy of your mercies.

O Lord, I know you yourself promise to be my greatest reward. You work in me, both to will and to do your good pleasure. Amen.

—John Wesley, *A Collection of Forms of Prayer
for Every Day in the Week,* 1738

A PRAYER TO LIVE AT THE HEART OF THINGS

God, Infinite Goodness, confirm your past mercies to me by empowering me for the rest of my life to act more faithfully than I have in the past. For the time I have left on earth, let me satisfy your command to love you totally.

Don't let me live under delusion:

> Do not let me rest in my outward devotion.
> Do not let me trust in works, sighs or tears.
> Do activate love for you.
> Do grace me with awareness of loving you with all my heart.

Amen.

—John Wesley, *A Collection of Forms of Prayer for Every Day in the Week,* 1738

A PRAYER FOR
CHURCH GROWTH

Accept the prayers and sacrifices of your holy church, offered to you.

Clothe your preachers with righteousness.

Pardon your people not prepared to worship you.

Prosper all sincerely engaged in propagating your faith and love.

Give your Son the unreached for his inheritance, and the furtherest reaches of the earth for his possession. Make your name great wherever the sun sets and rises.

Empower all of us in this nation, especially those who rule in church and state, to serve you in holiness and to know the love of Christ that passes understanding. Amen.

—John Wesley, *A Collection of Forms of Prayer for Every Day in the Week,* 1738

DO ANYTHING YOU WISH
WITH ME, LORD

my Father, my God, I live in your care; may I take joy above everything else in this fact.

Do with me what seems good in your sight. Only let me love you with all my mind, soul, and strength.

Amen.

—John Wesley, *A Collection of Forms of Prayer
for Every Day in the Week,* 1738

Week Forty-Six

OSovereign Good . . . you
order and govern all things, even
the most minute.

John Wesley

IN PRAISE OF THE SOVEREIGN GOD

Sovereign Good, I believe that in your mighty wisdom you order and govern all things, even the most minute, for your glory and the good of those who love you!

I believe, O Father of the families of heaven and earth, that you use all events to best magnify your goodness, to all your children, especially those whose eyes wait patiently to see you.

I humbly ask you to teach me to adore your ways, though I cannot comprehend them. Teach me to rejoice that you are king, to give you thanks for everything that comes to me.

For that which will come, give me your grace to do what pleases you; then, with absolute submission to your wisdom, help me to leave the results in your hand. Amen.

—John Wesley, *A Collection of Forms of Prayer for Every Day in the Week*, 1738

I SURRENDER. HELP!

O Lord Jesus, I give you my body,

> my soul,
>
> my possessions,
>
> my fame,
>
> my friends,
>
> my liberty,
>
> my life.

Use me and all I own as you wish. I do not belong to myself but to you.

> Claim me as your right.
>
> Keep me as your charge.
>
> Love me as your child.
>
> Fight for me when I'm wounded.
>
> Revive me when I'm destroyed!

Amen.

—John Wesley, *A Collection of Forms of Prayer for Every Day in the Week,* 1738

I GIVE GOD
(1) MY UNDERSTANDING

I give you my understanding. Grace me with a real intention to:

> Know you,
>
> Know your perfections,
>
> Know your works,
>
> Know your will.

Let everything else become nothing to me; only let me focus on the excellency of knowing about you.

Let me silence all false reasoning against what you teach me because you cannot deceive or be deceived.

Amen.

—John Wesley, *A Collection of Forms of Prayer for Every Day in the Week,* 1738

I GIVE GOD (2) MY WILL

I give you my will. I want not to will on my own.
Whatever you will, I want to will also. I want to will
your glory in all things, just as you do, and make that
the ultimate end of whatever I do.

I want to say with the psalmist, "Whom do I
have in heaven but you? I do not desire anyone on earth
but you."

Help me to delight when doing your will, and rejoice
in allowing you to help me do it.

Whatever threatens me, let me say, "The Lord acts in
this; let him do what seems good to him."

In whatever happens, let me give thanks because he
sends his will concerning me. I Thessalonians 5:18.

Amen.

—John Wesley, *A Collection of Forms of Prayer
for Every Day in the Week,* 1738

I GIVE GOD (3) MY EMOTIONS

I give you my emotions. Do what you will with them.

> You are my love,
>> my fear,
>> my joy.

Do not allow anything to share my emotions, but you.

> What you love, I want to love.

> What you hate, I want to hate.

And I want these feelings in the measure you prescribe them. Amen.

—John Wesley, *A Collection of Forms of Prayer for Every Day in the Week,* 1738

I GIVE GOD (4) MY BODY

I give you my body to
    Glorify you with it,
    Preserve it in purity,
    Live in it,
    Make it fit for you.
Do not let me
    Indulge it,
    Overuse it.
Do let me
    Keep it healthy,
    Maintain its vigor,
    Keep it active,
    Use it in whatever service you request.
Amen.

—John Wesley, *A Collection of Forms of Prayer for Every Day in the Week,* 1738

I GIVE GOD (5) MY POSSESSIONS

I give you all my worldly goods. Help me to
    Prize them, and
    Use them only for you.

May I faithfully give back to you what you have intrusted to me, by giving to the poor . . . especially what I own beyond necessities.

Grace me with contentment to part with material possessions, whenever you, my Lord, ask me to give them up.

Amen.

—John Wesley, *A Collection of Forms of Prayer for Every Day in the Week*, 1738

Week Forty-Seven

Save me, O God, as "a brand snatched out of the fire."

John Wesley

IN PRAISE OF THE CRUCIFIED CHRIST

Jesus, poor and abject, unknown and despised, have mercy on me, don't let me be ashamed to follow you.

O Jesus, hated, slandered, persecuted, have mercy on me, and don't let me be afraid to follow you.

O Jesus, betrayed and sold at a miserable price, have mercy on me, and make me content to live with you as my Master.

O Jesus, blasphemed, accused and wrongfully condemned, have mercy on me, and teach me to endure the contradiction of sinners.

O Jesus, clothed in reproach and shame, have mercy on me and don't let me seek my own glory.

O Jesus, insulted, mocked and spit upon, have mercy on me, and help me run with patience the race ahead.

O Jesus, dragged to the whipping post, scourged and bathed in blood, have mercy on me so that I do not faint in any fiery trial.

Amen.

—John Wesley, *A Collection of Forms of Prayer for Every Day in the Week*, 1738

A PRAYER TO CHRIST CRUCIFIED

Jesus, crowned with thorns,

    mocked in derision,

    burdened with our sins,

    burdened with the curses of the people,

    offended,

    outraged,

    insulted,

    overwhelmed with injuries, griefs and humiliations,

    hanged on the accursed tree,

    bowed down,

    sacrificed,

have mercy on me and conform my whole soul to your holy, humble, suffering Spirit.

    Amen.

—John Wesley, *A Collection of Forms of Prayer for Every Day in the Week,* 1738

IN GRATITUDE TO THE SAVING GOD

O how easy you forgive! Your nature is to forgive. How right for you to save! Salvation is your name.

How natural for you to come into the world! That's your business.

Even though I know I am the chief of sinners, I do not have to beg for you to save me. You, by nature, cannot leave me without grace. Thank you for having mercy on me.

Amen.

—John Wesley, *A Collection of Forms of Prayer for Every Day in the Week,* 1738

RECEIVE ME, MY SAVIOR

Receive me, my Savior, as a sheep gone astray but now returned to the Great Shepherd and Bishop of my soul.

Father, accept my imperfect repentance, love me in spite of my ailments, forgive my wickedness, purify my uncleanness, strengthen my weakness, fix my unstableness and let your good Spirit watch over me forever. I want your love, always, to rule in my heart. Do this by the merits of the sufferings and love of your Son in whom you always find pleasure.

Amen.

—John Wesley, *A Collection of Forms of Prayer
for Every Day in the Week,* 1738

I'LL PRAISE MY MAKER

I'll praise my Maker while I've breath,
And when my voice is lost in death,
   Praise shall employ my nobler powers.
My days of praise shall ne'er be past,
While life and thought and being last,
   Or immortality endures.

—John Wesley's *Charlestown Collection of
Psalms and Hymns*, 1737;
this hymn, originally by Isaac Watts,
was altered by John Wesley.

O FOR A SHOUT OF SACRED JOY

O for a shout of sacred joy
    To God the sovereign King!
Let every land their tongues employ,
    And hymns of triumph sing.

While angels shout and praise their King
    Let mortals learn their strains:
Let all the earth his honors sing;
    O'er all the earth he reigns.

—John Wesley's *Charlestown Collection of*
Psalms and Hymns, 1737

THE CHRISTIAN RACE

Awake our souls (away our fears,
Let every trembling thought be gone);
Awake, and run the heavenly race,
And put a cheerful courage on.

True, 'tis a straight and thorny road,
And mortal spirits tire and faint:
But we forget the mighty God,
That feeds the strength of every saint.

O mighty God your matchless power
Is ever new, and ever young,
And firm endures while endless years
Their everlasting cycles run.

From you the overflowing spring
Our souls shall drink a fresh supply;
While those who trust their native strength
Shall melt away, and droop and die.

Swift as an eagle cuts the air
We'll mount aloft to your abode;
On wings of love our souls shall fly
Nor tire along the heavenly road!

—John Wesley's *Charlestown Collection of
Psalms and Hymns,* 1737

Week Forty-Eight

❧

I believe three things must go together for our justification:

1. God's part: his great mercy and grace.
2. Christ's part: the satisfaction of God's justice by offering his body and shedding his blood, and fulfilling the law of God perfectly.
3. Our part: true and living faith in the merits of Jesus Christ.

John Wesley

HOW GOD JUSTIFIES US

To express my meaning a little more, I believe three things must go together for our justification:

1. God's part: his great mercy and grace.

2. Christ's part: the satisfaction of God's justice by offering his body and shedding his blood, and fulfilling the law of God perfectly.

3. Our part: true and living faith in the merits of Jesus Christ.

In our justification, God not only exercises his mercy and grace, but his justice also. The grace of God does not shut out the righteousness of God in our salvation, but only shuts out the righteousness of ourselves, i.e., the righteousness of our works.

—John Wesley, *The Principles of a Methodist,* 1742

ONLY TRUE AND LIVING FAITH

Strictly speaking, neither my faith nor my works save me. God himself creates my faith so he can forgive my sins.

God justifies. He does this of his own mercy through the merits of his Son only.

Once given, faith enables me to embrace the promise of God and forgiveness. In that context, the Scripture says faith, not works, justifies.

Therefore we must renounce any self-created "faith," our own works and our virtues. Our corruption because of original sin rears its head so forcefully that mere human faith, love, words and works cannot help us in any way to get justified.

All this humbles us before God and gives Christ all the glory for our salvation.

—John Wesley, *The Principles of a Methodist,* 1742

BUT TRUE FAITH DOES GOOD WORKS

We must also observe that the faith that justifies us issues in good works. "Faith" that does not yield good works is not true faith. Even the devils believe in the Virgin Birth of Christ, miracles, the Incarnation, his death, his ascension into heaven, and that he will come again to earth to judge the quick and the dead.

All this the devils believe, along with everything else written in the Old and New Testaments. But for all this "faith" they remain devils, damned, lacking true *Christian* faith.

—John Wesley, *The Principles of a Methodist,* 1742

SURE TRUST AND CONFIDENCE

The true Christian faith relates not only to belief in the Holy Scriptures and the Articles of our Faith,* but also a sure trust and confidence of personal salvation from everlasting damnation.

From this trust and confidence comes a loving heart to obey his commandments. No devil has this faith, nor any wicked person either.

—John Wesley, *The Principles of a Methodist,* 1742

* Official beliefs of the Church of England (Episcopal)

FAITH'S DOUBLE FRUIT

Peter Böhler told me two fruits come from faith in Christ: dominion over sin and constant peace from a sense of forgiveness.

This amazed me back then and I looked upon this as a new gospel.

—John Wesley, *The Principles of a Methodist,* 1742

PETER BÖHLER'S SIX RESULTS

1. When one has living faith in Christ, justification results.
2. This justification always comes from God in a moment.
3. In that moment one has peace with God.
4. One cannot have his peace without knowing it.
5. Born of God, the one saved quits sinning.
6. This deliverance from sin one cannot have without knowing it.

—John Wesley, *The Principles of a Methodist*, 1742

ASSURANCE

believe that justification is the same thing as new birth. One may have full assurance of sins forgiven, yet not be able to tell the hour or day when he or she received this full assurance, because it may grow in the mind by degrees.

—John Wesley, *The Principles of a Methodist,* 1742

Week Forty-Nine

What are the distinguishing
marks of the people
called Methodists?

John Wesley

WHAT THEN IS THE MARK?

Who is a Methodist?

A Methodist is one who has the love of God filling the heart. This comes by the Holy Spirit.

One who loves the Lord God with all the heart, with all the soul, and with all the mind and strength—that one is a Methodist.

God becomes the joy of the heart, and the desire of the soul. This makes the soul cry out, "I desire only God in heaven or earth. My God! My all! You are the strength of my heart, and all I need forever!"

—John Wesley, *The Character of a Methodist*, 1742

METHODIST ARE HAPPY PEOPLE

Methodists, therefore, are happy in God. They are always happy, because in them a well of water springs up to eternal life. That spring overflows in the soul with peace and joy.

Perfect love has cast out fear and brings joy. Methodists rejoice in the Lord always, in God their Savior.

—John Wesley, *The Character of a Methodist,* 1742

METHODISTS WANT TO PRAY, NOT FAINT

Methodists pray without ceasing. They have been assigned to pray, not faint.

Not that they always go to a house of prayer, though they neglect no opportunity to go.

Not that they always go to their knees, though they often kneel.

Not that they cry aloud to God in words always, for often the Spirit intercedes with groans that cannot come to words.

But at all times the language of a Methodist's heart says, "I lift my heart to God." That's the essence of prayer.

—John Wesley, *The Character of a Methodist*, 1742

METHODISTS LOVE OTHERS AS THEMSELVES

Those who love God love their neighbors also. They love neighbors as themselves. They love all people.

They do not have to know people personally to love them. Nor do they have to approve of people to love them. Methodists love their enemies; they repay hate with goodwill. If they cannot do something good, they continue to pray, even if the enemies still treat them badly and persecute them.

—John Wesley, *The Character of a Methodist*, 1742

METHODISTS AIM AT
A PURE HEART

The love of God purifies the heart from all revenge, envy, malice, wrath, every unkind emotion or feeling. God cleanses from pride and haughtiness, from which comes contention.

God gives mercy, kindness, humility of mind, meekness, and patience. God enables one to put up with a great deal and to forgive people who want to quarrel.

Methodists want to desire only God.

—John Wesley, *The Character of a Methodist,* 1742

METHODISTS DO NOT LOVE THE WORLD

Methodists do not love the world or any of the things of the world. They want to be crucified to the world, and the world crucified to them.

Dead to the world, to the lust of the flesh, the lust of the eye, and the pride of life. All desire focuses in God.

—John Wesley, *The Character of a Methodist*, 1742

METHODISTS WANT TO DO GOOD

Methodists do good to all people: neighbors, strangers, friends, and enemies. And that in every possible way:

> Feeding the hungry,
>
> Clothing the naked,
>
> Visiting the sick and imprisoned.

Methodists do even more, to do good to their souls:

> Awakening those who sleep in death,
>
> Bringing the awakened to the cross to get peace,
>
> Prodding those who have peace to have more love and show that love in good works.

Methodists show willingness to spend, and be spent, in service to God.

—John Wesley, *The Character of a Methodist,* 1742

Week Fifty

Hark, my dull soul,
how every thing
Strives to adore our generous King!
Hark, each a double tribute pays:
First sings its part and then obeys.

John Wesley

THE ARMOR OF GOD

Soldiers of Christ, arise,
And put your armor on,
Strong in the strength which God supplies
Through his eternal Son;
Strong in the Lord of hosts,
And in his mighty power,
Who in the strength of Jesus trusts
Is more than conqueror.

Stand then in his great might,
With all his strength endued,
And take, to arm you for the fight,
The weaponry of God;
That having all things done,
And all your conflicts past,
You may o'ercome through Christ alone,
And stand entire at last.

—Appears at the end of Wesley's
Character of a Methodist, 1742

A BETTER RELIGION

We see—who does not?—the countless follies and miseries of our fellow creatures. We see on every side either persons of no religion, or people of lifeless, formal religion. This grieves us.

We would greatly rejoice, if by any means, we could convince some of a better religion, a religion no other than love, the love of God for all persons. To love the God who first loved us with all our heart, soul and strength forms the basis of all good, all hope.

—John Wesley, *An Earnest Appeal to Men of Reason and Religion*, 1743

THE MEDICINE OF LIFE

This love of God and all persons we believe to be the medicine of life, the never-failing remedy for all the evils of a disordered world. Love cures all miseries and vices.

Wherever one finds love, one also finds virtue and happiness of mind, gentleness, long-suffering, the whole image of God and at the same time the peace that passes all understanding, along with joy unspeakable and full of glory.

—John Wesley, *An Earnest Appeal to Men of Reason and Religion,* 1743

ETERNAL SUNSHINE

ternal sunshine of the spotless mind;
Each prayer accepted, and each wish resigned:
Desires composed, affections ever even,
Tears that delight, and signs that waft to heaven.

—Alexander Pope, quoted in John Wesley's
*An Earnest Appeal to Men of
Reason and Religion,* 1743

THE RELIGION WE LONG TO SEE

This is the religion we long to see established in the world, a religion of love and joy and peace, having its seat in the heart and in the inmost soul, but ever showing itself by its fruits continually springing up not only in all innocence (for love works no ill to neighbor), but also in every kind of good by spreading virtue and happiness all around it.

—John Wesley, *An Earnest Appeal to Men of Reason and Religion,* 1743

HOW TO UNDERSTAND THE THINGS OF GOD

This is the way to understand the things of God: "Meditate on them day and night." In this way you will attain the best knowledge, even to "know the only true God, and Jesus Christ whom he sent."

This knowledge will lead you "to love him, because he first loves us." And when you love God with your total being, will you not then have "that mind in you which was also in Christ Jesus"? And in consequence of this, while you joyfully experience all the holy tempers, you will also behave in a holy way and in your talk, too.

—John Wesley's Preface to *Explanatory Notes Upon the Old Testament*, 1765

A SIXFOLD MEDITATION PATTERN TO HELP YOU

If you desire to read the Scriptures to learn to understand the things of God, let me suggest this pattern:

1. Set apart a little time each morning and evening.

2. Try to find time to read a chapter of the Old Testament and a chapter from the New; if you haven't that much time, read a single chapter or part of one.

3. Read with focus to know the whole will of God and with fixed resolution to do it.

4. As you read notice how faith connects with the grand doctrines: original sin, justification by faith, the new birth, and inward and outward holiness.

5. Pray earnestly before reading because Scripture can be understood only through the Spirit. Also close your reading with prayer, so that what you read may be written in your heart.

6. While you read, pause once in awhile, asking if you really do believe and then live out what the Scriptures say.

Whatever you learn and resolve to do, begin to do it the first moment you can; in this way the Word actually becomes the power of God in present and eternal salvation.

—John Wesley's Preface to *Explanatory Notes Upon the Old Testament*, 1765

Week Fifty-One

Let reason do all
that reason can.

John Wesley

THE SON OF GOD OPENS
OUR EYES

The Son of God begins his work by enabling us to believe in him. He both opens and enlightens the eyes of our understanding. Out of darkness he commands light to shine, and takes away the veil that the "god of this world" put over our hearts. We then see, not by a chain of *reasoning* but by a kind of *intuition*, by a direct view, that "God was in Christ reconciling the world to himself."

—John Wesley's sermon, "The End of
Christ's Coming," 1781

WHERE'S THAT LIGHT NOW?

I remember clearly the *light* you had on real scriptural Christianity. You saw what heart-religion meant. . . . You had earnest desires to experience the whole gospel. And you evidenced the sincerity of those desires by the steps you took in your family. In everything you hastened to be not almost but altogether a Christian.

Where's that *light* now?

Do you now see that true religion is not a negative or external affair, but the life of God in the soul of man, the image of God stamped on the heart? Do you now see that in order to have this, Jesus Christ, of his own free will, puts us right before a just God and redeems us? What happened to the desires after you felt the hungering and thirsting after right living? And where are the marks of a soul really pleading for God and refusing comfort from anything less than his love?

—John Wesley, *Letters*, to James Knox, May 30, 1765

GOD'S GIFT OF REASON

ou go on: "It is a fundamental principle, in the Methodist school, that all who join must renounce their reason."

Sir, are you awake? Unless you are talking in your sleep, how can you utter so gross an untruth? It is a fundamental principle with us that to renounce reason is to renounce religion, that religion and reason go hand in hand, and that all irrational religion is false religion.

—John Wesley, *Letters,* to Dr. Rutherforth, 1768

THE DESIRE FOR KNOWLEDGE

The desire for knowledge lies in all people, stemming from in our inmost nature. Not a variable, we find it in every rational person unless suspended by some stronger desire.

We also find it insatiable: "The eye is not satisfied with seeing, nor the ear with hearing"; nor the mind with any degree of knowledge.

More, God planted the desire for knowledge in every soul for excellent purposes. It hinders our taking up rest in anything here below; it lifts our thoughts to higher and higher objects, more and more worthy of our consideration, until we ascend to the Source of all knowledge and excellence, the all-wise, all-gracious Creator.

—John Wesley's sermon, "The Imperfection
of Human Knowledge," 1784

KNOWLEDGE HAS BOUNDARIES

Though our desire for knowledge has no bounds, knowledge itself has. Indeed, confined to boundaries, it narrows far more than common people imagine. More than people with learning acknowledge this, too.

Here we have a strong intimation (since the Creator does nothing in vain) that some future state of being will satisfy our insatiable thirst for knowledge. That desire satisfied, we will no longer experience such an immense distance between the appetite for learning and the achievement of it.

—John Wesley's sermon, "The Imperfection of Human Knowledge," 1784

LET REASON DO WHAT IT CAN

Let reason do all that reason can. Employ it so far as it will go. But at the same time acknowledge reason's total incapability of giving faith, or hope, or love, and consequently of producing real virtue or substantial happiness.

Expect these from a higher source, the Father of the spirits of all flesh. Seek and receive them, not as your own acquisition, but as the gift of God. Lift up your hearts to him who "gives to all liberally." He alone can give faith, "the evidence" and conviction "of things not seen." He alone can bring you the "lively hope" of an inheritance eternal in the heavens. He alone can "shed his love abroad in your heart by the Holy Spirit given you."

—John Wesley's sermon, "The Case of Reason
Impartially Considered," 1781

REASON ASSISTED BY
THE HOLY SPIRIT

Reason, unassisted by the Holy Spirit, will not give you the understanding Holy Scripture declares about the being and attributes of God: his eternity and bigness, his power, wisdom and holiness.

Reason does help us in some measure to comprehend his method of dealing with people; reason helps us see the nature of his work during the old- and new-covenant periods, and of the law and gospel.

Reason also helps us comprehend how his Spirit opens and enlightens our eyes so that we can understand repentance, the faith that saves us and the nature and condition of justification with its immediate and subsequent fruits. We also learn, by reason, to define the new birth without which we cannot enter the kingdom of heaven. It helps us see that holiness without which no one shall see the Lord. By the good use of reason, we come to know what inward and outward holiness means —that is, the mind of Christ and the meaning of walking as Christ walked.

—John Wesley's sermon, "The Case of Reason
Impartially Considered," 1781

Week Fifty-Two

How does he "bear witness with our spirit that we are children of God"?

John Wesley

THE WITNESS OF THE SPIRIT

What is the testimony of God's Spirit? How does he "bear witness" to our spirits that "we are children of God"? It is hard to find language to explain "the deep things of God." Indeed, we will find no words that will adequately express what the children of God experience.

Perhaps, one might say, the testimony of the Spirit is an inward impression on the soul, whereby the Spirit of God directly witnesses to my spirit, that I am a child of God. The Spirit tells me Jesus Christ loves me, that he gave himself for me and that all my sins are blotted out. I, even I, am reconciled to God.

> —John Wesley's sermon, "The Witness
> of the Spirit, I," 1746

THE BOOK OF NATURE

he world around us is the mighty volume wherein God declared himself. Human languages differ in different nations; those of one nature, written in a universal language, every person can read.

The book of nature consists not of words, but things which picture the divine perfections. The earth and sky, with all the stars, declare the immensity and magnificence, the power and wisdom, of its Creator. Thunder, lightning, storms, earthquakes and volcanos show the terror of his wrath. Seasonable rains, sunshine and harvest, denote his big and good heart, and demonstrate how he opens his hand and fills all living things plentifully.

The constantly succeeding generations of plants and animals imply the eternity of their first cause. Life in millions of different forms shows the vast diffusion of this animating power, and death the infinite disproportion between him and every living thing.

—John Wesley, *Letters,* to Dr. Conyers Middleton, 1749

ANIMALS POINT TO GOD

The actions of animals form an eloquent and feeling language. Those that want the help of persons have a thousand engaging ways which, like the voice of God speaking to the heart, command us to preserve and cherish them.

The motions or looks of the animals that might harm us strike terror and warn us either to flee from or arm ourselves against them.

So every part of nature directs us to nature's God.

—John Wesley, *Letters*, to Dr. Conyers Middleton, 1749

UPWARD MOVEMENT

The whole progress of nature is so gradual that the entire chasm from a plant to a person is filled with all kinds of creatures rising, one above another, by so gentle an ascent that the transitions from one species to another are almost indiscernible. And the intermediate space is so well cared for that there is hardly a degree of perfection that does not appear somewhere.

Now, since the ladder of creation advances, by regular steps as high as humankind, is it not probable that it still proceeds gradually upwards through beings of a superior nature? There is an infinitely greater space between the Supreme Being and people than between people and the lowest insect.

—John Wesley, *A Compendium of Natural Philosophy,* 1777

THE BOOK OF GOD

O that I, like Timothy,
  Might the Holy Scriptures know,
From my earliest infancy,
  Till for God mature I grow,
Made unto salvation wise,
Ready for the glorious prize.

Jesus, all-redeeming Lord,
  Full of truth, and full of grace,
Make me understand your Word,
  Teach me in my youthful days
Wonders in your Word to see,
Wise through faith that is in you.

Open now my eyes of faith,
  Open now the Book of God,
Show me here the secret path,
  Leading to your bless'd abode:
Wisdom from above impart,
Speak the meaning to my heart.

—John Wesley, *Poetics:* "Before Reading Scripture," 1763

THE ALL-POWERFUL GOD

God is all-powerful as well as present everywhere. His power has no boundaries. He "has a mighty arm; strong is his hand, and high is his right hand." He does whatever pleases him in the heavens, the earth, the sea, and in all deep places.

With people we know many things are impossible, but not with God, for with him, "all things are possible." Whenever he wills, he can do right now what he wishes.

—John Wesley's sermon, "The Unity of the Divine Being," 1789

GOD AND ETERNITY

ow can God, who inhabits eternity, stoop to regard creatures of a day, persons whose lives pass away like a shadow?

This thought has struck many serious minds, as it did David's, and creates a kind of fear lest God forget them; this God who grasps all space and all eternity. But doesn't this fear arise from the supposition that God is really like ourselves? If we consider boundless space or boundless duration, we shrink into nothing before it. But God is not a human being.

A day, or millions of ages, amount to the same with him. Therefore, whenever that thought recurs, whenever you suffer temptation to fear lest you should go forgotten before the immense, the eternal God, remember that nothing stands little or great, that no time span appears long or short to him.

—John Wesley's sermon, "On Eternity," 1786

NOTES

NOTES